michael
Schwalberg

S0-CNG-558

TREATING BULIMIA

Pergamon Titles of Related Interest

Bellack/Hersen DICTIONARY OF
BEHAVIOR THERAPY TECHNIQUES

Blanchard/Andrasik MANAGEMENT OF CHRONIC
HEADACHES: A Psychological Approach

Blechman/Brownell BEHAVIORAL MEDICINE FOR WOMEN

Kanfer/Goldstein HELPING PEOPLE CHANGE:
A Textbook of Methods, Third Edition

Kirschenbaum/Johnson/Stalonas TREATING CHILDHOOD
AND ADOLESCENT OBESITY

Related Journals *

ADDICTIVE BEHAVIORS
CLINICAL PSYCHOLOGY REVIEW
WOMEN'S STUDIES INTERNATIONAL FORUM

*Free sample copies available upon request

PSYCHOLOGY PRACTITIONER GUIDEBOOKS

EDITORS
Arnold P. Goldstein, Syracuse University
Leonard Krasner, SUNY at Stony Brook
Sol L. Garfield, Washington University

TREATING BULIMIA
A Psychoeducational Approach

LILLIE WEISS, Arizona State University
MELANIE KATZMAN, New York Hospital
SHARLENE WOLCHIK, Arizona State University

PERGAMON PRESS
New York   Oxford   Toronto   Sydney   Frankfurt

Pergamon Press Offices:

U.S.A.	Pergamon Press Inc., Maxwell House, Fairview Park, Elmsford, New York 10523, U.S.A.
U.K.	Pergamon Press Ltd., Headington Hill Hall, Oxford OX3 0BW, England
CANADA	Pergamon Press Canada Ltd., Suite 104, 150 Consumers Road, Willowdale, Ontario M2J 1P9, Canada
AUSTRALIA	Pergamon Press (Aust.) Pty. Ltd., P.O. Box 544, Potts Point, NSW 2011, Australia
FEDERAL REPUBLIC OF GERMANY	Pergamon Press GmbH, Hammerweg 6, D-6242 Kronberg-Taunus, Federal Republic of Germany

Copyright © 1985 Pergamon Press Inc.

Library of Congress Cataloging in Publication Data

Weiss, Lillie.
    Treating bulimia.

    (Psychology practitioner guidebooks)
    Bibliography: p.
    Includes index.
    1. Appetite disorders--Treatment. 2. Psychotherapy
I. Katzman, Melanie. II. Wolchik, Sharlene.
III. Title. IV. Series. [DNLM: 1. Appetite Disorders--
therapy. 2. Psychotherapy. WM 175 W429t]
RC552.A72W45   1985   616.85′2   85-3478
ISBN 0-08-032400-2
ISBN 0-08-032399-5 (pbk.)

All rights reserved. No part of this publication may be reproduced, stored in a retrieval system or transmitted in any form or by any means: electronic, electrostatic, magnetic tape, mechanical, photocopying, recording or otherwise, without permission in writing from the publishers.

Printed in Great Britain by A. Wheaton & Co. Ltd., Exeter

To Dr. Joseph Masling,
who has directly or indirectly influenced
each one of us, for introducing us to the
link between eating and emotions and for
his continued encouragement over the years

Contents

Preface

The orgiastic consumption of food followed by purging, once considered merely a footnote to the history of ancient Rome, has recently begun to receive attention as a clinical phenomenon. This increase in awareness has resulted in rising numbers of women seeking treatment for this aberrant pattern of eating termed bulimia. Unfortunately, many mental health professionals asked to provide these services are uninformed as to the characteristics and treatment of persons with this syndrome. Despite a recent flurry of professional articles on the area, there still is no comprehensive theory of bulimia. Thus both research and treatment of this disorder have proceeded in a haphazard, unsystematic manner. In view of the demand for treatment, however, many clinicians have attempted to treat bulimia with few guidelines on how to proceed.

Several years ago, we became interested in learning how bulimia developed so that we could design a program to help binge eaters and purgers. We wanted to see how bulimic women were different from binge eaters and non-binge eaters. We found that bulimic women had several common personality characteristics in addition to their disturbed eating behaviors. Other researchers have also found certain personality deficits to be associated with bulimia. Despite the awareness of the clinical features associated with bulimia, no treatment program for this disorder has systematically addressed them in its approach.

We designed a treatment program for bulimia based on the research findings and have used it with groups and individuals with very encouraging results. We have continued to refine our program, and our purpose in writing this book is to help the clinician who is working with bulimic women individually or in groups. The 7-week, self-enhancement program described in this book is short-term and can easily be adapted by most clinicians.

Acknowledgments

We could not have written this book without the women who have participated in our program. We would like to thank them for sharing with us their most intimate thoughts and feelings, which provided us with the information on which much of this book is based, and for their patience in filling out our questionnaires—again and again and again.

We are also indebted to Dr. Paul Karoly, Director of Clinical Training, Department of Psychology, at Arizona State University, for his invaluable help in the publication of this book. We appreciate the special effort he made to help us publish this book, as well as his support and encouragement through our successes and disappointments.

We would like to thank Dr. Alex Zautra, Director of the Clinical Psychology Center at Arizona State University, and the rest of the staff there for their support and enthusiasm for our program. We thank Wendy Ramerth and Gina Sherman at the Clinical Psychology Center for their assistance and Fran Beynon for deciphering our illegible scribbles and transforming them into a readable workbook, as well as for all her work in the program.

Special thanks goes to Sandra McDill for typing this manuscript and for her cheerful meeting of deadlines. We also thank Lynn Fisher and Karen Katzman for their legal assistance.

We also wish to thank Mr. Jerome Frank of Pergamon Press for his help and suggestions and for making working on this book so pleasurable. Thanks to Angela Piliouras also for all her help in the production of our book.

Chapter 1
Introduction

This chapter presents an overview of bulimia, including a description of the syndrome and its effects, as well as a review of the research findings on its etiology and treatment. The chapter also discusses the research on which the authors' treatment program is based and the rationale for that program. Although the handbook is intended primarily for the clinician, a review of the research findings on this eating disorder is important because media reports on the syndrome have sensationalized it and have blurred the distinction between fact and myth. In addition, this chapter provides an outline of the rest of the book and an introduction to the treatment program.

DEFINITION

In 1980, "bulimia," literally "ox hunger," was included as a diagnostic entity in the *Diagnostic and Statistical Manual III (DSM III)* (APA, 1980). The features of bulimia include episodic eating patterns involving rapid consumption of large quantities of food in a discrete period of time, usually less than 2 hours; awareness that this eating pattern is abnormal; fear of being unable to stop eating voluntarily; and depressed mood and self-deprecating thoughts following the eating binges. The presence of three of the following are also needed: eating in private during a binge; termination of a binge through sleep, social interruption, self-induced vomiting, or abdominal pain; repeated attempts to lose weight by self-induced vomiting, severely restrictive diets, or use of cathartics and/or diuretics; and frequent weight fluctuations due to alternating binges and fasts. In addition, the bulimic episodes must not be due to anorexia nervosa or any known physical disorder (APA, 1980).

Unfortunately, the *DSM III* criteria were developed after work on this disorder had begun. Therefore, the use of the term "bulimia" has been confusing. For example, bulimia has been used to describe both a symptom (binge eating) and a syndrome. As a symptom, the term bulimia has been used to describe binge eating in subgroups of patients with anorexia nervosa (Casper, Eckert, Halmi, Goldberg, & Davis, 1980; Garfinkel, Moldofsky, & Garner, 1977) and to describe an eating pattern in patients who are overweight or obese (Loro & Orleans, 1981; Stunkard, 1959). Whether these groups of patients bear any clinical similarities to people with bulimia who are of normal weight is not clear. As a syndrome, bulimia has been studied under a variety of different names, which makes interpretation of the literature difficult. In addition to the *DSM III* label bulimia, terms include thinfats (Bruch, 1973), bulimarexia or binge-starvers (Boskind-Lodahl, 1976; Boskind-Lodahl & Sirlin, 1977), bulimia nervosa (Rosen & Leitenberg, 1982; Russell, 1979), vomiters and purgers (Beumont, George, & Smart, 1976), and compulsive eaters (Green & Rau, 1974). Additionally, there has been much media distortion as to what constitutes bulimia. When we use the term, we are referring primarily to women of average weight who are suffering from the *DSM III* defined *syndrome*, bulimia.

EPIDEMIOLOGY

Although binge eating and purging has been considered a rare disorder (Bruch, 1973), recent studies suggest increased frequency in both clinical and college samples. Stangler and Printz (1980) reported that 3.8% of college students treated at a university psychiatric clinic were bulimic, using the *DSM III* criteria. They considered this to be a ''strikingly frequent'' diagnosis, one which was significantly more common among women than men. In other, more recent research with female college students, prevalence figures for bulimia have ranged from 3.9% to 19% (Halmi, Falk, & Schwartz, 1981; Katzman, Wolchik, & Braver, 1984; Pyle, Mitchell, Eckert, Halvorson, Neuman, & Goff, 1983). Johnson, Lewis, Love, Lewis and Stuckey (1983), who report one of the few studies on a non-college population, found that 8.3% of high school females met *DSM III* criteria for bulimia.

Although these figures suggest that bulimia occurs in a high percentage of women, these estimates mostly pertain to college populations. Little information exists for the general population. Another problem with these estimates is that there are few objective diagnostic criteria. Researchers differ on the definition of a binge, as well as on the frequency required to distinguish normal binge eating levels from pathological levels. Also at issue is the inconsistency of including ''purging'' in a working definition; some researchers have used purging in their definition, whereas others have not. Researchers have found that prevalence estimates decreased from 4.5% to 1.0% for female college students (Pyle et al., 1983) when criteria were changed from weekly binge eating to weekly binge eating *and* weekly vomiting or laxative use.

The fact that bulimic behaviors typically occur in private, followed by feelings of guilt or shame, may account for an additional proportion of unidentified bulimics, and several authors caution that their findings may underestimate prevalence due to patients' reluctance to report their eating disorder (Halmi et al., 1981; Stangler & Printz, 1980). Although the number of published reports dealing with bulimia has increased considerably in the last few years, it is not known whether this increase parallels an increase in the frequency of the disorder or whether it merely indicates that patients with the disorder are just now receiving professional attention (Mitchell & Pyle, 1981).

In addition to studying the prevalence of women meeting *DSM III* definition of bulimia, several authors have examined the occurrence of binge eating. These studies suggest that binge eating is common. Prevalence figures have ranged from 54% to 86% for college women (Halmi et al., 1981; Hawkins & Clement, 1984; Katzman et al., 1984; Ondercin, 1979). The definition in most prevalence studies has generally been a "yes" response to the question "Do you binge eat?" or variations thereof. Hawkins and Clement (1984) asked their subjects, "Do you ever binge eat?" Halmi et al. (1981) asked, "Have you ever had an episode of eating an enormous amount of food in a short space of time (an eating binge)?" Katzman and Wolchik (1984) asked "Do you binge eat?", and Ondercin (1979) asked, "Would you label yourself a compulsive eater (i.e., overeating without regard to actual physical hunger)?" When a stricter definition of binge eating was employed (for example, binge eating at least eight times in the past month) the prevalence estimate dropped to 7.2% (Katzman et al., 1984). Although several researchers have studied the personality and behavioral characteristics of binge eaters (Dunn & Ondercin, 1981; Hawkins & Clement, 1984), the similarity in symptomology between women who report binge eating and bulimics is unclear and has been addressed in only one study (Katzman & Wolchik, 1984). Although it is possible that therapists may treat binge eaters, normal weight women who report binge eating are less disturbed by their eating habits than bulimics and less likely to seek therapy (Katzman & Wolchik, 1984).

Descriptions of the typical bulimic have been remarkably similar across studies. The average bulimic can be characterized as a white, single, college-educated woman from an upper- or middle-class family (Fairburn & Cooper, 1982). The age of onset is commonly in the late teens (Fairburn & Cooper, 1982; Johnson & Berndt, 1983; Katzman & Wolchik, 1984; Leon, Carroll, Chernyk, & Finn, 1985; Russell, 1979; Pyle, Mitchell, & Eckert, 1981), with a duration of about 4 (Leon et al., 1985; Pyle et al., 1981; Russell, 1979) to 5 (Fairburn & Cooper, 1982; Johnson, Stuckey, Lewis, & Schwartz, 1982) years before the woman first seeks treatment (Johnson et al., 1982; Russell, 1979; Pyle et al., 1981). Many of these women have a history of disordered eating. Katzman and Wolchik (1984), Leon et al.

(1985), Pyle et al. (1981), and Russell (1979) reported that at least 33.3% of their samples had histories of extreme weight loss, whereas Johnson et al. (1982) reported that 50% of their sample had a history of being overweight. In almost every case the women were struggling to obtain a below normal ideal weight (Katzman & Wolchik, 1984; Leon et al., 1985; Pyle et al., 1981; Russell, 1979; Weiss & Ebert, 1983). Although bulimics view their eating habits as abnormal, many learned the binge/purge behaviors from friends or from the media (Fairburn & Cooper, 1982; Katzman & Wolchik, 1984). Once a woman begins the binge-purge cycle, she commonly continues to experience hunger, is preoccupied with food, and feels guilty after a binge (Katzman & Wolchik, 1983; Leon et al., 1985; Mizes, 1983; Pyle et al., 1981; Russell, 1979). These women also generally maintain a normal weight (Abraham & Beumont, 1982; Johnson et al., 1982).

Whereas the eating habits of bulimic women often enable them to maintain a normal weight, they also produce other, less desirable results. In three studies of normal weight bulimics, subjects described their eating pattern as very disruptive of their daily lives (Johnson et al., 1982; Katzman & Wolchik, 1983; Leon et al., 1985). Clinicians also note that this eating pattern can have serious effects, citing interference with social relationships and school or job performance (Leon et al., 1985; Pyle et al., 1981; Wooley & Wooley, 1981), as well as medical problems such as urinary tract infection (Russell, 1979), gastric dilation (Mitchell, Pyle, & Miner, 1982), parotid gland swelling (Levin, Falko, Dixon, & Gallup, 1980), electrolyte abnormalities (Mitchell & Pyle, 1981), hair breakage, amenorrhea (Johnson et al., 1982; Pyle et al., 1981), destruction of dental enamel (House, Grisius, & Bliziotes, 1981), and fatigue (Abraham & Beumont, 1982; Johnson et al., 1982).

TOPOGRAPHY OF BINGE EATING

Behavioral Description

Although information on the cognitive and affective antecedents and consequences of binge eating is limited, several researchers have investigated binge eating behavior. The frequency of binge eating episodes varies widely across studies; however, approximately 50% of the bulimic women in treatment sampled in studies by Johnson et al. (1982), Leon et al. (1985), and Pyle et al. (1981) reported binge eating at least daily. Studying 14 normal weight nonclinical bulimic women, Katzman and Wolchik (1982) reported a mean of 23 binges a month. Using a predominantly normal weight clinical sample, Mitchell, Pyle, and Eckert (1981) reported a mean of 11.7 binges per week, with a range of 1–46 episodes. The caloric intake during binges has been reported to range from 1,200 calories

(Mitchell et al., 1981) to 55,000 calories (Johnson et al., 1982). Katzman and Wolchik (1983a) and Leon et al. (1985) reported an average consumption of 2,500 calories per binge in samples of normal weight bulimics. On the average, women report spending $8.30 per binge (Johnson et al., 1982), with some spending as much as $70.00 per binge (Wooley & Wooley, 1982).

Data on the frequency of binges and total caloric intake during binges are difficult to interpret. These data are retrospective and, in most reports, the binge is not clearly differentiated from food consumed during meals. Additionally, although consumption of large amounts of food is most common, patients may label consumption of small amounts of a forbidden food (i.e., one cookie) as a binge (Leitenberg, Gross, Peterson, & Rosen, 1984; Mizes, 1983).

Five investigations have described the details of binge eating behavior (Johnson et al., 1982; Katzman & Wolchik, 1983; Leon et al., 1985; Mitchell et al., 1981; Pyle et al., 1981). Across these reports, the mean duration of a binge was roughly 1 hour. The majority of women reportedly binged alone and preferably at home. Women generally ate late in the day, or at night, and consumed foods that were highly caloric and required little preparation (for example, ice cream, candy, and doughnuts). The food consumed during a binge often included items that the women would not typically eat given their dieting concerns (Abraham & Beumont, 1982).

In addition to the binge eating itself, bulimics display other eating disturbances. They frequently alternate between binge eating and periods of very low food consumption or fasting (Loro & Orleans, 1981; Weiss & Ebert, 1983). Pyle et al. (1981) reported that bulimics frequently do not eat for more than 24 hours after a binge and then find themselves famished, thereby prompting another binge. Bulimics may also fail to eat in a systematic manner (e.g., three meals a day) on the days they do eat (Leon et al., 1985; Mizes & Lohr, 1983).

It is interesting to note that studies on the eating habits of binge eaters reveal behaviors similar to bulimics (Crowther, Lingswiler, & Stephens, 1983; Hawkins & Clement, 1984; Katzman & Wolchik, 1983; Ondercin, 1979). However, the groups differ on the frequency of binge eating and the use of purging to counteract the caloric intake.

Data on the purging aspect of bulimia suggest that the use of evacuation techniques follows the onset of binge eating from 1 (Fairburn & Cooper, 1982; Johnson et al., 1982) to 4 (Katzman & Wolchik, 1984) years. Vomiting was reported in 94%, 92%, 83%, and 81% of the women in studies by Pyle et al. (1981), Mitchell et al. (1981), Fairburn and Cooper (1982), and Johnson et al. (1982), respectively. Across these studies, approximately 50% of the women who vomited did so daily. About 50% of the women in these four studies also abused laxatives. Johnson et al. (1982) reported that of the women who used laxatives, 24.5% did so daily. Diuretics, enemas, and appetite suppressants were also employed for weight control, although not as frequently. Johnson et al. (1982) also reported that of those women who did not currently exhibit purging behavior, 79.4% were tempted to do so.

Emotions and Cognitions

Two different methodologies have been employed to gain information on the antecedents and consequences of binge eating, namely, retrospective reporting by bulimic women and naturalistic self-monitoring. Both Abraham and Beumont (1982) and Leon et al. (1985) asked normal weight women in treatment for bulimia or binge eating to recall their feelings before and after binge eating. Women in both studies indicated that they ate when feeling anxious or depressed. Similar results were found in nonclinical samples of binge eaters. Both Crowther et al. (1983) and Ondercin (1979) reported that binge eating episodes were associated with the negative affective states, anxiety and depression. Pyle et al. (1981), however, found that only 18% of the women in their study reported anxious feelings prior to eating.

The effect of binges on these negative emotional states has also been studied. Binge eating has positive reinforcement aspects in terms of the pleasant taste of food and relief from pre-binge negative emotional states (Loro & Orleans, 1981). Ondercin (1979) found that the questionnaire item "eating seems to calm me down or make me feel better" was the best predictor of binge eating on a stepwise multiple regression analysis. Leon et al. (1985) reported reductions in depression and anger during the binge and reductions in anxiety, depression, and feeling driven to eat shortly after the binge. Whereas Abraham and Beumont (1982) reported that 100% of the women in their study ate to reduce tension, only 66% indicated that they felt relieved from anxiety after a binge. These data tentatively suggest that although some women may eat to relieve anxiety, many do not achieve the desired relief.

Although some emotional states appear to decrease during or after the binge, others increase, mainly in the post-binge period. Both Leon et al. (1985) and Pyle et al. (1981) report that most bulimics related negative emotions such as anger, disgust, and guilt when asked about their feelings following a binge. Rosen and Leitenberg (1982) have hypothesized that these post-binge negative emotional states serve as a cue for purging, which allows the binger to reverse the eating act, thus decreasing negative affect caused by the binge eating itself.

Several studies have employed naturalistic self-monitoring to assess the cognitive and affective states associated with binge eating. Johnson and

Larson (1982) used an innovative method to explore the impact of binge eating and purging episodes on various affective states among bulimics. Fifteen bulimic women were given electronic pagers to wear for 1 week. The pagers were used to signal participants at various times of the day to complete a self-report questionnaire on their situations and emotional states at those times. The data suggest that uncontrolled eating, possibly once employed as a means of modulating negative mood states, becomes a stimulus for more negative feelings once women realize that they are out of control.

Katzman and Wolchik (1983a) also conducted a naturalistic assessment of the affective cognitive and behavioral antecedents and consequences of binge eating. A nonclinical college sample of 12 bulimic women completed self-monitoring forms for 4 days or four binges, whichever came first. The self-monitoring data indicated that binge eating was often precipitated by food-oriented thoughts accompanied by anxious or depressive affective states. School-related events, such as poor grades or exams, often occurred prior to the binge. Following binge eating, many women felt out of control and negatively about themselves. In addition, relief and/or negative emotions such as anger or guilt frequently occurred.

In summary, both the historical and self-monitoring data gathered on normal weight bulimics tentatively suggest that binge eating episodes are precipitated by feelings of anxiety and negative emotional states, as well as by hunger. They also suggest that the binge eating, initiated in response to tension or negative affect, does not successfully alleviate the bulimic's negative state.

PERSONALITY AND
BEHAVIORAL CHARACTERISTICS

Only two studies have compared normal weight bulimics (recruited from a university community) with controls on a number of standardized measures (Katzman & Wolchik, 1984; Weiss & Ebert, 1983). Katzman and Wolchik (1984) compared the personality and behavioral characteristics of 30 women who met the *DSM III* criteria for bulimia with those of 22 women who reported binge eating but did not fulfill these criteria and with 28 controls. The measures used included: the Herman and Polivy Restraint Scale (1978), the Hawkins and Clement Binge Scale (1980), the Rosenberg Self Esteem Index (1979), the Levenson and Gottman Dating and Assertion Questionnaire (1978), the High Self Expectations and Demand for Approval subscales of the Jones Irrational Beliefs Test (1968), the Kurtz Body Attitude Scale-Evaluation Dimension (1970), the Beck Depression Inventory (Beck, Ward, Mendelson, Mock, & Erbaugh, 1961), and the Personality Attributes Questionnaire (Spence, Helmreich, & Stapp, 1979). In comparison with both binge eaters and controls, bulimics were more depressed and had lower self-esteem, poorer body image, higher self-expectations, higher need for approval, greater restraint, and higher binge scores. No significant differences were found on measures of dating, assertion, or sex-role orientation.

Weiss and Ebert (1983) compared 15 normal weight *DSM III* bulimics to 15 controls using the Symptom Check List (SCL) (Deragotis, Lipman, & Covi, 1973), the Piers-Harris Self-Esteem Scale (1969), the Nowicki-Strickland Locus of Control Scale (1973), the Maudsley Obsessive-Compulsive Inventory (Rachman & Hodgson, 1980), the Holmes and Rahe Social Readjustment Scale (1967), the Social Network Index (Berkman & Syne, 1979), the Goldberg Anorectic Attitude Scale (1980), and the Goldberg Situational Discomfort Scale (1978). In comparison with controls, bulimics reported themselves to have significantly more psychopathology on all nine symptom dimensions of the SCL-90—somatization, obsession-compulsion, interpersonal sensitivity, depression, anxiety, anger, phobic anxiety, paranoid ideation, and psychoticism. Bulimics also exhibited a greater external locus of control, rated themselves as more compulsive, expressed greater fear of fat, and indicated more anxiety in situations related to eating than controls. Measures of social adjustment and support were not significantly different between groups.

The results reported by both Katzman and Wolchik (1984) and Weiss and Ebert (1983) offer substantial evidence of pathology in normal weight bulimics. Their finding that bulimia in a nonclinical population coexists with personality deficits is supported by large scale research on bulimics seeking treatment. Both Fairburn and Cooper (1982) and Johnson et al. (1982) noted greater depression for bulimics when compared with the mean for a normal population. In addition, Fairburn and Cooper (1982) reported high scores for anxiety, while Johnson et al. (1982) reported high scores on interpersonal sensitivity.

There is a great deal of research suggesting that bulimia and depression are related. Russell (1979) reported that after preoccupation with eating, dieting, and weight, depressive symptoms are most prominent with bulimia. Herzog (1982), using *DSM III* criteria for depression, found that 75% of the bulimic women reported significant depressive symptoms. Johnson and Larson (1982), investigating the emotional experiences of bulimics and normals, found that bulimics experience significantly more negative mood states, notably depression and anxiety. In another study, Johnson et al. (1983) found that bulimics scored significantly higher than normals on depression on the Hopkins Symptom Checklist. In addition, more than half of the sample reported they often felt depressed and over half reported a history of suicidal ideation. Also, 5% had attempted suicide, indicating significant psychological distress. Similarly, studies employing the Minnesota Multiphasic Personality Inventory (MMPI) (Hatsukami, Owen, Pyle, & Mitchell, 1982; Leon et al., 1985; Pyle et al., 1981; Ross, Todt, & Rindflesh, 1983) have found elevations or near elevations of the Depression Scale (Scale 2) for bulimics.

The studies that have reported a decrease in bulimic symptoms using antidepressants (Pope, Hudson, Jonas, & Yurgetun-Todd, 1983; Walsh, Stewart, Wright, Harrison, Roose, & Glassman, 1982) lend further support to the contention that bulimia and depression are related. There has not been sufficient research in the area to warrant any firm conclusions, but studies of family history (Pyle et al., 1981; Hudson, Laffer, & Pope, 1982) and of response to the dexamethasone suppression test (Hudson et al., 1982) have demonstrated a similarity between patients with bulimia and patients with major depression.

Consistent with the findings that bulimics are depressed, there is evidence to suggest that the life adjustment of bulimics is poor. Johnson and Berndt's (1983) findings indicated that bulimics had a poorer life adjustment in the areas of work, social and leisure activities, and family relations compared with a normal community sample.

Although bulimics frequently report a desire to be thinner than their current weight (Leon et al., 1985; Katzman & Wolchik, 1984; Pyle et al., 1981; Russell, 1979), little research has been conducted on the bulimics' perceived weight. Ruff (1982) compared bulimics' judgments of physical dimensions to normals by asking subjects to adjust the size of a light line projected on the wall to represent the width of five body areas. Even though the groups did not differ on actual physical dimensions and both groups were within 10% of ideal weight, bulimics overestimated their physical dimensions significantly more than controls. This comparison with normal females is important because college females generally feel that their ideal weight is lower than their current weight (Katzman & Wolchik, 1984). The importance of perceived weight to bulimia is further highlighted by Halmi et al. (1981), who found that a belief that they weighed more than their actual weight distinguished those who fulfilled bulimic criteria from those who did not.

Although many researchers have suggested that the bulimics' difficulties in interpersonal relationships are most salient in their dealings with the opposite sex, little systematic research has been done in this area. The only available information comes from two studies that employed weak criteria and unstandardized measures. However, the results of these studies will be reported because they suggest important areas for future research. Rost, Neuhaus, and Florin (1982) and Allerdisson, Florin, and Rost (1981) found that when compared with matched controls, women who reported eating binges followed by purges were significantly less "liberated" in both sex-role attitudes and behavior. The eating disordered group also showed a significant attitude-behavior gap, with sex-role behavior being more traditional than sex-role attitudes (Rost et al. 1982). Binge-purgers also indicated less enjoyment of sexual relationships, more difficulty in expressing sexual wishes, and more fear of not meeting partners' sexual expectations. In addition, these women expressed the belief that their enjoyment of sex would improve if they were slimmer and more attractive (Allerdisson et al., 1981). The finding by Rost et al. (1982) that bulimics endorsed significantly more traditional sex-role attitudes than controls differs from the results of Katzman and Wolchik (1984). However, the differences in assessment measures and group definition may account for this discrepancy. Clearly, more research on this variable is needed.

Several studies have suggested that bulimics have a difficulty with impulse control as reflected by self-reports of stealing (Leon et al., 1985; Pyle et al., 1981; Russell, 1979), alcohol use (Leon et al., 1985; Pyle et al., 1981), and drug use (Leon et al., 1985 ; Russell, 1979). However, these studies failed to compare bulimics with controls. When bulimics were compared with controls on use of alcohol and cigarettes, no significant differences were found (Katzman & Wolchik, 1984). This finding is consistent with the findings of Johnson et al. (1982), who reported infrequent drug, alcohol, and cigarette use among 316 bulimics.

Four studies have assessed the Minnesota Multiphasic Personality Inventory (MMPI) scores of bulimics and have found remarkably similar results (Hatsukami et al., 1982; Leon et al., 1985; Pyle et al., 1981; Ross, Todt, & Rindflesh, 1983). Across studies, the findings were elevations or near elevations of the Depression Scale (Scale 2), Psychopathic Deviate Scale (Scale 4), Psychasthenia Scale (Scale 7), and Schizophrenia Scale (Scale 8). Notably low scores have been found on the Masculinity-Femininity Scale (Scale 5). Overall, these findings are representative of significant depression, anxiety and worry, feelings of alienation and impulsivity.

Leon et al. (1985) specifically commented on the masculinity-femininity scores. This score represents concern about physical attractiveness and passive, home-oriented pursuits (Lachar, 1974). Of particular interest is the general findings of high psychopathic deviate and low masculinity-femininity scores. This profile is characterized by overemphasis on the stereotypic female role, including an excessive concern about appearance. People obtaining these elevations need affection and are easily hurt. Heterosexual dissatisfaction and/or dysfunction is common (Lachar, 1974).

These MMPI findings are consistent with previously discussed research suggesting that bulimics suffer from anxiety and depression, have a high need for approval, experience sex role difficulties, have problems with impulse control, and place an overemphasis on physical appearance. Overall, these MMPI results lend even greater support to the notion that bulimia occurs with personality and behavioral deficits. Although these studies provide a first step in understanding the personality characteristics correlated with the development of bulimia, they provide no information on the role of stress or limited coping ability as an etiological variable.

BULIMIA AND COPING

At present, the relationship between bulimia and stress can only be extrapolated from clinical impressions and patients' self-reports. Clinical researchers such as Fairburn have noted that bulimic behavior represents "a difficulty coping with disturbing feelings and thoughts in patients who rely on binge eating as a means of relieving distress" (Fairburn, 1982, p. 631). This view is shared by Mitchell and Pyle, who indicated that "many patients who binge-eat do not seem to do so in response to hunger, [and] in some individuals the phenomenon appears to be related to stress" (Mitchell & Pyle, 1981, p. 70), and by Lacey, who reported that "bulimic bouts of overeating become more frequent or more violent when the patient is emotionally stressed" (Lacey, 1982, p. 62).

Loro and Orleans (1981) and Gormally (1984) suggested that, because binge eating provides immediate negative reinforcement in that it reduces high levels of tension, eating acquires the power to relieve stress and becomes a habit that is difficult to break. Many clinicians concur with this view and add that binge eating is further complicated by some women's lack of alternative coping mechanisms. Although the binge eating may provide temporary relief from anxiety states, in some cases the overeating leads to a subsequent increase in negative feelings. As a result, the emphasis of some women's struggle becomes the disordered eating rather than the factors that initially elicited the stress (Fairburn, 1982; Hawkins & Clement, 1984; Stunkard, 1959; Wilson, 1978).

As mentioned previously, researchers have suggested that within this context, bulimia continues to be a mechanism of adaptation and coping, although not a very effective one (Coffman, 1984; Hawkins & Clement, 1984; Mizes, 1983; Ondercin, 1979). Although the hypothesis of limited coping skills has often been repeated, a review of the literature reveals only two studies on the relation between disordered eating patterns and coping strategies. Hawkins (1982) assessed 340 female undergraduates of varying weights on coping styles and eating behavior. Although his study tentatively suggests that eating behavior may be correlated with coping style, because of the many methodological problems it is difficult to generalize the results to normal weight bulimic women. Katzman's (1984) study suggests that bulimics may not exhibit a unique coping style when compared with other women with frequent binge eating or depression. Her findings also suggest that bulimics may not demonstrate a lack of coping strategies but rather the inability to select styles that they can use effectively. Alternatively, it is possible that bulimic women possess the appropriate coping resources but fail to see their coping attempts as effective. This study suggests that treatment for the bulimic may need to focus on refining existing coping strategies other than eating and/or altering the bulimic's evaluation of her ability to handle difficult situations.

THEORIES OF ETIOLOGY

Biological, psychological, and social factors have been hypothesized to play a role in the development of bulimia. Drawing upon clinical and experimental experience, researchers have given different emphasis to each of these factors in developing etiological models. This section will review the various theories of etiology and conclude with a discussion of the empirical support for existing theoretical models.

Boskind-Lodahl (1976) was one of the first to develop a theory of etiology for bulimia. Based on her clinical observations of 36 female clients seen at a university mental health clinic, she hypothesized that an overacceptance of the feminine stereotype was causal in bulimia. She speculated that the pursuit of thinness reflects perfectionist strivings to achieve an ideal of femininity through which the bulimic hopes to gain the approval of others and validate her own self-worth. As well as striving to perfect and control their physical appearances, these women display a strong need for achievement in other areas. According to Boskind-Lodahl, the binge-purge behavior, which begins as a means of dieting, may generalize into a tension reduction strategy in the face of concerns about sexuality, dating, and achievement. "For the person who is struggling to meet unrealistic goals by imposing severe and ascetic control over herself, the binge is a release" (Boskind-Lodahl, 1976, p. 351).

This theory of etiology has served as a point of departure for other researchers who also view the development of bulimia from a psychosocial perspective. Based on research conducted with college students who reported binge eating, Hawkins and Clement (1984) have suggested that cultural expectations for weight consciousness are particularly salient to females and that compliance with these expectations causes a constant pursuit of thinness. Binge eating results only when there is the addition of certain "pathogenic predispositions" that are biological, such as an elevated "set point" for body fat (Nisbett, 1972), or cognitive, such as a distorted body image. The co-action of these pathogenic predispositions and the psychosocial pressure result in a particular personality pattern, which includes low self-esteem, compulsive rigidity, dieting as a high priority, preoccupation with food, and a histrionic fear of loss of control of eating. In addition, Hawkins and Clement (1984) suggest that bulimics have depressive tendencies and perceive themselves as socially incompetent. Within this context, Hawkins (1982) has suggested that the binge is best understood using a stress-coping framework that examines the "person by environment fit." Hawkins hypothesizes that the college life-style poses a tension between work orientation and dieting concerns for late adolescent females. Drawing upon the depression literature (i.e., Coyne, Aldwin, & Lazarus, 1981), Hawkins suggests that unpleasant events and "daily hassles," such as rejection in romantic relationships or academic difficulties, may precipitate overeating mediated by a faulty cognitive approval of the stressor. The bulimic's negative assessment of the event may result in a sense of loss of control over the stressor. Feeling helpless to change the situation, the bulimic turns to food hoping that "eating will make me feel better." Underlying this model are several assumptions: (a) binge eating is seen as part of an on-going coping process; (b) binge eaters have a faulty cognitive appraisal of stressors and experience events as more negative than non-binge eaters; (c) binge eaters hold irrational beliefs and are less efficient in cognitive problem solving than non-binge eaters; and (d) effective treatment strategies must involve the acquisition of alternative, positive coping strategies (Hawkins, 1982).

Although Hawkins presents an elaborate model, most of his hypotheses and assumptions lack empirical validation. In a preliminary study, Hawkins (1982) reported the results of an assessment battery distributed to 340 female undergraduates of varying weights. Included in this battery were measures of coping styles, negative life events, eating attitudes, and weight fluctuations. Women obtaining high scores on the Eating Attitudes Test (EAT) (Garner & Garfinkel, 1979), a measure of diet preoccupation and loss of control over eating, reported significantly more negative life events. Also, high scores on the restrictive diet subscale of the EAT were significantly positively correlated with the use of problem-solving and social-support seeking coping strategies. In contrast, high scores on the loss of control or bulimic tendencies subscale were significantly positively correlated with the use of passive, inner-directed coping mechanisms. However, none of the scales of the coping measure were correlated with weight fluctuation.

Although this study tentatively suggests that attitudes toward eating may be correlated with coping style, its many methodological problems make it difficult to generalize the findings to normal weight bulimics. First, it is unclear how many of the women in the sample were bulimic or even reported binge eating. The only assessment of disordered eating was a high score on a scale of "bulimic tendencies." Also, the author reported that the women were of varying weights and did no· elaborate further. Thus, the number of subjects who were underweight, overweight, or normal weight is unclear. In addition, the psychometric properties of the coping assessment battery, developed by the author, are unknown. Clearly, more work needs to be done to assess the utility of this model.

Based upon clinical experience and a review of the literature on bulimia, Mizes (1983) has proposed a model for bulimia that draws heavily upon the theories of Boskind-Lodahl (1976) and Hawkins and Clement (1984). This model emphasizes that irrational beliefs and self-control deficits are central to the pathogenesis of the disorder. Mizes suggests that the familial environment may foster certain irrational beliefs and may over endorse traditional female sex roles. He hypothesized that a familial emphasis on passivity and the need for a man to take care of a woman may inhibit the bulimic's development of global self-management skills. In addition, irrational beliefs, such as excessive need for approval (e.g., "everyone must like me or I am worthless") or high self-expectations, are hypothesized to give rise to many interpersonal difficulties such as assertion deficits, sex role disturbance, and body image distortion. These factors may lead to poor heterosexual relationships in which sex is distressing or dysfunctional. Irrational beliefs may also cause the bulimic to evaluate her self-worth and her dieting behavior according to overly perfectionist standards. The combination of high self-expectations and poor self-management skills may result in either actual or perceived failure and subsequent anxiety or depression, which precipitate binge eating. "At least one potential reason for the bulimic's almost exclusive reliance on binging as a coping strategy is her general deficit in self-control coping strategies" (Mizes, 1983, p. 34).

Contrary to Hawkins and Clement (1984) and Mizes (1983), who hypothesized that strained relationships and ineffective methods of handling tension lead to binge eating, Wooley and Wooley (1981) suggested a reverse relationship between these factors. Based on clinical experience with six bulimics, they hypothesized that young women with histories of weight concern discover vomiting as a means of weight control and a way to reduce the anxiety caused by eating. For these women, college represents freedom from parental observation, increased access to food, and greater psychological pressures. The pattern gradually shifts from vomiting after meals to planned episodes of secret eating. For some women the entire sequence becomes identified as a generalized means of reducing anxiety.

Wooley and Wooley (1981) liken this excessive food intake to regulate tension to a form of substance abuse. They view bulimia as similar to other addictive behaviors in which an individual develops a tolerance, indulging in increasingly greater amounts of food, and in which there is deterioration of life-style and personal relationships because the habit requires more and more time and money to support it. However, unlike other addictions, there is no subculture of users; instead, food abuse generally occurs in private.

Wooley and Wooley (1981) do not believe that learning alone can account for the remarkable similarities among case histories, which leads them to suggest that the "understanding of this disorder is to be found primarily in study of the physiology of the regulation of food intake and the conditioning of anxiety reduction" (Wooley & Wooley, 1981, p. 50).

Similarly, Russell (1979) stated that pathophysiological mechanisms interact with psychological mechanisms in the development of bulimia. His model is based on case materials and prospective observations of 30 bulimic women, 24 of whom had a history of anorexia nervosa. In his view, some psychological disorder leads the woman to reject her "healthy" weight and to opt for a thinner ideal. Urges to eat result in emotional distress, and fear of weight gain leads to vomiting or laxative use after overeating. Vomiting and/or laxative use keeps the weight at a reduced level, a suboptimal weight that may produce electrolyte disturbance, gastric dilation, renal failure, urinary infections, and most importantly, hypothalamic disturbances. Russell postulated that the hypothalamus responds to the suboptimal body weight by triggering bouts of overeating. This hypothalamic response may also play a part in influencing attitudes toward food either during or before eating. Although Russell's model fails to specify the exact nature of the emotional and hypothalamic disturbance, it does highlight the self-perpetuating mechanisms involved in this disorder.

An alternative perspective is offered by Rosen and Leitenberg (1982) and Leitenberg, Gross, Peterson, and Rosen (1984). Their model, which is based on clinical experience with five bulimics, suggests that binge eating and self-induced vomiting are linked in a vicious cycle by anxiety. Similar to Russell (1979), these authors have suggested that bulimics harbor a morbid fear of weight gain. Eating elicits this anxiety whereas vomiting following food intake reduces anxiety. Vomiting for the bulimic is viewed as having an anxiety reducing function similar to compulsive rituals such as hand washing and lock-checking in obsessive-compulsive neuroses. Thus vomiting, rather than binge eating, is considered to be the driving force in bulimia. A person who fears gaining weight might not binge eat if the food could not be expelled afterwards. This model focuses exclusively on the eating behavior and is restricted to women who purge following a binge.

The view that purging is the major factor in the maintenance of bulimic behavior is shared by Johnson and Larson (1982), who present a model based on their research with 15 bulimic patients. They concur with Wooley and Wooley's (1981) suggestion that uncontrolled eating may best be understood as an addictive behavior; however, they believe that bulimia develops in an attempt to modulate dysphoric mood states. They suggest that a combination of predisposing factors, including biochemical and familial variables, may influence the bulimic's selection of food as a mechanism of tension reduction. However, in response to the cultural emphasis on thinness for women, bulimics use evacuation techniques as a protection against the stigma of becoming overweight. Johnson and Larson (1982) hypothesize that over time, unrestrained eating leads to a sense of loss of control and begins to elicit its own negative affective states. At this point, a transformation occurs whereby purging behavior replaces binge eating as the primary mechanism for tension reduction.

Two common themes are apparent in each of these theoretical models. First, each theory suggests that bulimics may differ from controls in more than just their eating habits, and that bulimia may develop against a backdrop of deficits in personality and behavioral characteristics. Second, with the exception of Russell (1979), each theory suggests that the reduction of anxiety becomes an important factor in the maintenance of this aberrant eating behavior. However, the pervasiveness of the binge/purge cycle as a tension regulator differs across models. Restricting their theorizing to bulimics who purge, Rosen and Leitenberg (1982) suggest that the purge response develops as a means of controlling the stress elicited by feelings of hunger and subsequent eating. According to their model, treatment for the bulimic would best be focused on coping with the anxiety of eating. Contrary to this opinion, Hawkins and Clement (1984), Johnson and Larson (1982), and Mizes (1983) suggest that binge eating and/or purging may serve a broader tension reducing function and is used as a means of reducing anxiety for women with limited coping abilities. It follows from these latter theories that treatment must be aimed at the development of alternative means of reducing stress or anxiety.

The studies reviewed in the previous section on the personality characteristics of bulimics provide some empirical support for various components of these theoretical models. The suggestion made by Boskind-Lodahl (1976), Hawkins and Clement (1984), and Mizes (1983) that bulimic women demonstrate an overidentification with the feminine stereotype and difficulties in heterosexual relationships is supported by studies employing the MMPI (Hatsukami et al., 1982;   Leon et al. (1985) ; Pyle et al., 1981; Ross et al., 1983) and other measures of sex-role attitudes (Allerdisson et al., 1981; Rost et al., 1982). Similarly, the hypothesis that bulimics hold irrational beliefs such as an excessively high need for approval and perfectionist standards (Boskind-Lodahl, 1976; Mizes, 1983) was supported by Katzman and Wolchik (1984). The suggestion in all of these models that dieting is a high priority was also supported (Katzman & Wolchik, 1984; Weiss & Ebert, 1983) as was the observation by Mizes (1983) and Hawkins and Clement (1984) that bulimics have a poor body image (Katzman & Wolchik, 1984; Weiss & Ebert, 1983). In addition, the hypothesis that bulimics display depressive tendencies (Hawkins & Clement, 1984; Johnson & Larson, 1982) received empirical validation (Fairburn & Cooper, 1982; Katzman & Wolchik, 1984; Johnson et al., 1982; Weiss & Ebert, 1983).

After a careful review of the literature, we have used previous research and theories (Beck, 1967; Boskind-Lodahl, 1976; Coyne, Aldwin & Lazarus, 1981; Hawkins & Clement, 1984; Russell, 1979; Wooley & Wooley, 1981) to design our own empirically based model for the development of bulimia. This model includes two interacting, positive feedback loops. As shown in Figure 1.1, two factors contribute to the bulimic cycle. First is the extreme dieting behavior, subsequent binge eating, and purging. The second factor is the bulimic's ineffective use of both food and alternative coping strategies to deal with stressful academic and interpersonal situations. According to our model, certain personality characteristics such as poor body image, low self-esteem, high need for approval, high self-expectations, and depression predispose women to develop maladaptive methods of weight control when confronted with societal pressure to conform to a thin ideal. Initially these women engage in highly restrictive dieting that ultimately results in binge eating and difficulty maintaining a low body weight. Purging may begin as an attempt to counteract the weight gain, but when women view their eating habits as out of their control and abnormal, greater depression, lower self-esteem, and anxiety result. These negative mood states lead to a further increase in binge eating. The above mentioned personality deficits are also associated with how women cope with interpersonal academic stressors. When stressed, bulimics use binge eating and/or purging as one method of stress reduction. In addition to binge eating, bulimics use many other coping behaviors, few of which are evaluated as effective. Although binge eating provides a temporary distraction from anxiety, this behavior causes additional tension for bulimics who view their eating habits as abnormal, disruptive, and physically harmful. The inability to cope successfully exacerbates their low self-esteem, depression and anxiety, and leads to further binge eating. In addition, increased difficulty handling stressful situations and a more negative evaluation of their coping behaviors ensue.

Our model suggests that bulimia occurs with personality and behavioral deficits as well as with ineffective coping strategies, and that treatment programs need to address cognitive, affective, and behavioral problems as well as the dysfunctional eating patterns. Our treatment package was designed specifically to address each of these deficits in a systematic manner. Before describing our treatment program, we will review some of the current treatments for bulimia.

TREATMENT

Despite the increasing awareness of bulimia and its negative psychological and physical consequences, there has been very little written on the treatment of this disorder. In the past, bulimic symptoms have been

FIGURE 1.1. Diagram of a Working Model of Bulimia[1]

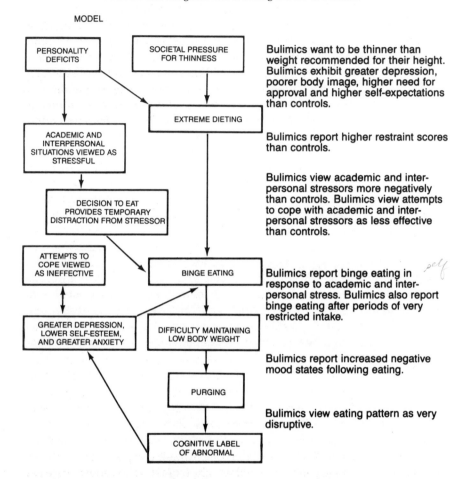

MODEL

Bulimics want to be thinner than weight recommended for their height. Bulimics exhibit greater depression, poorer body image, higher need for approval and higher self-expectations than controls.

Bulimics report higher restraint scores than controls.

Bulimics view academic and interpersonal stressors more negatively than controls. Bulimics view attempts to cope with academic and interpersonal stressors as less effective than controls.

Bulimics report binge eating in response to academic and interpersonal stress. Bulimics also report binge eating after periods of very restricted intake.

Bulimics report increased negative mood states following eating.

Bulimics view eating pattern as very disruptive.

[1]An earlier version of this model was presented by Katzman and Wolchik (1983b).
[2]Data supporting this model are provided by Katzman and Wolchik (1983), Katzman and Wolchik (1984), and Katzman (1984).

treated as part of more general approaches to weight control or anorexia nervosa. In general, there has not been a correspondence between proposed etiologies and treatment approaches. Treatment has included hospitalization (Garfinkel & Garner, 1982; Russell, 1979), pharmacological approaches using anticonvulsants (Green & Rau, 1974; Weiss & Levitz, 1976; Greenway, Dahms, & Bray, 1977; Wermuth, Davis, Hollister, & Stunkard, 1977) or antidepressants (Hudson et al., 1982; Walsh et al., 1982; Pope et al., 1983), behavior therapy (Kenny & Solyom, 1971; Rosen & Leitenberg, 1982), cognitive behavioral treatment (Fairburn, 1981; Linden, 1980; Long & Cordle, 1982), and group therapy (Boskind-Lodahl & White, 1978; White & Boskind-White, 1981).

Many of the existing treatment studies have often been limited to small samples, usually single-case studies (e.g., Grinc, 1982; Kenny & Solyom, 1971; Linden, 1980; Long & Cordle, 1982; Rosen & Leitenberg, 1982), and most of the available studies have methodological problems (cf. Mizes, 1983) that make it difficult to generalize from them. These methodological weaknesses have included uses of quasi-experimental designs, use of treatment packages that preclude causal inferences to specific procedures, as well as measurement problems. In addition, most of the treatment programs have focused primarily on the modification of the binge eating and/or purging (e.g., Grinc, 1982; Kenny & Solyom, 1971; Leitenberg et al., 1984; Mizes & Lohr, 1983) rather than the behavioral deficits that coexist with this disorder. A description of some of the treatment approaches used with bulimics follows.

Pharmacological Treatment

Pharmacological studies have investigated the use of anticonvulsant and antidepressant medications for treating bulimia. The results of the studies using anticonvulsants have been mixed. Green and Rau (1974) reported 90% success using the anticonvulsant diphenylhydantoin. However, the criteria for success were not specified. Wermuth et al. (1977) found only 40% of their subjects reported some improvement. Other researchers (Weiss & Levitz, 1976; Greenway et al., 1977) have found that anticonvulsant medication had no effect on binge eating.

Bulimia has been seen as a form of an affective disorder that may respond to antidepressant treatment (Hudson et al., 1982; Walsh et al., 1982). Hudson et al., however, provide no treatment data. Walsh et al. used monoamine oxidase inhibitors with six bulimic women and reported an improvement in eating behavior. However, they do not describe how this improvement was measured. Furthermore, the use of monoamine oxidase inhibitors with bulimics is problematic because it requires the elimination of certain foods from a diet, as ingestion of these foods along with the drug can have serious side effects. Bulimics, with their chaotic eating habits, may not adhere to a strict dietary regimen and may experience the negative side effects as a result. Pope et al. (1983) used imipramine with 22 bulimic women and found it effective in reducing the frequency of binge eating.

Behavioral Treatment

The majority of treatment studies have been behavioral studies, although those are broadly defined to encompass cognitive behavioral approaches. Most of these studies, however, have been limited to a small sample size. Many of these studies have focused mainly on the vomiting response.

Rosen and Leitenberg (1982) have used a behavior therapy approach to prevent the vomiting response. They treated a female university student, using an exposure plus prevention model of intervention. During every session, the bulimic ate until she experienced a strong urge to vomit, at which time her therapist had her focus her attention on her discomfort until the urge to vomit disappeared. Treatment with this woman was quite successful. She ceased vomiting on the 44th day of treatment with only one relapse during the 10-month follow-up. Prior to treatment, she had binged and vomited on a daily basis.

Johnson, Schlundt, Kelley, and Ruggiero (1984) also used exposure with response prevention to reduce vomiting frequency in a sample of six women. Inconsistent self-monitoring and the small sample size, however, limit definite conclusions about this treatment.

Kenny and Solyom (1971) reported successful treatment of vomiting behavior using an aversive conditioning approach. The subject was instructed to formulate a mental "still life" of each of the steps leading to vomiting and received electroshock to her middle finger as she pictured the image. The woman stopped vomiting after the 15th session and had not resumed at the 3-month follow-up.

Other behavior therapy strategies have included systematic desensitization (O'Neill, 1982) with three bulimics to reduce the anxiety associated with consumption of "forbidden" high caloric foods. The results for the three women were mixed. One showed only slight improvement at the end of treatment but a more dramatic decrease in binge eating at follow-up, another showed the reverse pattern, and the third ceased binge eating and maintained her gains at follow-up.

Linden (1980) describes a multicomponent behavioral treatment of a bulimic woman. In this case, the components of behavior therapy included assertiveness training, developing alternative food choice responses, stimulus control, and response delay. The woman had ceased vomiting and overeating after 9 weeks and maintained this at a 6-month follow-up.

Grinc (1982) has used a cognitive behavioral model in the treatment of a 26-year-old bulimic. In addition to stimulus control techniques, such as avoiding foods and situations related to vomiting and self-monitoring of behavior, Grinc used a technique involving cognitive restructuring of the woman's beliefs about vomiting. The woman showed a steady decrease in vomiting and ceased vomiting altogether after beginning cognitive restructuring. She maintained her therapeutic gains for the most part during the 1-year follow-up period.

Fairburn (1980) also reported the use of a cognitive behavioral approach for the treatment of bulimia. The treatment had two focuses: behavioral and cognitive. The behavioral aspects of the intervention required the bulimic woman to self-monitor her food intake and explore alternative responses. The cognitive focus of the intervention focused on changing maladaptive attitudes. Fairburn (1981) reported promising results with 11 women, using this cognitive therapy approach.

Long and Cordle (1982) describe an individualized therapeutic approach using behavioral techniques with cognitive modeling and dietary education. They provide case studies of two clients who ceased binge eating after 7 and 32 treatment sessions, respectively.

As we can see from the studies described so far, the majority of investigations have been behaviorally oriented, with few measuring personality characteristics that may occur along with the eating disorder. Many authors have provided working models for the treatment of bulimia (Coffman, 1984; Gormally, 1984) and suggest interventions that focus on more than the circumscribed eating response. Gormally states that bulimia has more to do with effective living and less to do with eating. Similarly, Coffman stresses the importance of *not* focusing on the binge-purge behaviors exclusively.

Multifaceted Group Treatment Approaches

Of the investigations that have included attention to behavioral deficits as well as to the maladaptive eating pattern (e.g., Boskind-Lodahl & White, 1978; Fairburn, 1981; Johnson, Connors, & Stuckey, 1983; Linden, 1980; Long & Cordle, 1982; White & Boskind-White, 1981), only one (Boskind-Lodahl & White, 1978) has employed a control group. Using a multifaceted treatment approach that included attention to social competence, sex-role stereotypes, acceptance of one's body image, and problems with one's parents as well as behavioral techniques of self-monitoring and contingency contracting, Boskind-Lodahl and White (1978) reported few significant effects of treatment relative to a no-treatment group. This ''experiential-behavioral'' approach to the treatment of bulimia is also described in a later study (White & Boskind-White, 1981) that did not employ a control group. In this study, binge eating decreased or ceased in 10 of 14 cases.

The authors suggest that bulimia is more than simply an eating disorder. They feel it is a "struggle to achieve a perfect, stereotypic female image in which women surrender most of their self-defining powers to others" (p. 501). Given the promising outcomes reported by Boskind-Lodahl and White (1978) as well as other researchers who have used broad based treatments in a less controlled manner (e.g., White & Boskind-White, 1981; Fairburn, 1981; Johnson et al., 1983), additional controlled studies in this area are clearly needed.

Several other studies have used a group treatment approach with bulimia. Roy-Byrne, Lee-Benner, and Yager (1984) conducted a yearlong therapy group with nine bulimics using combined behavioral and psychodynamic approaches. In this group format, group members kept diaries of their eating habits. In addition, therapy focused on cognitive restructuring of thoughts as well as some social skills training. By the end of the year, six had ceased or decreased their binge eating. However, no systematic description of the group program is offered and no control group was used. The authors emphasize the importance of group treatment in that it provides an opportunity for interpersonal learning, education, and receiving support.

Lacey (1983) also describes a group program for controlling bulimia. Relative to a no-treatment group, the women in the treatment group showed a significant improvement in binge eating. Although no systematic description of the program is provided, it appears that some attention is given to factors other than the eating behavior. The group is described as "insight oriented" and helping the patient to "deal herself with emotional and relationship problems." Although the therapists in this case had "knowledge of psychiatric patients and psychiatric methods," they had "no specialist training in group techniques" (p. 1610).

Johnson et al. (1983) treated 10 bulimic patients in a 12-session psychoeducational format. A more detailed description of their sessions is provided than in the previous two studies mentioned. The treatment consisted of three phases. The first phase focused on self-monitoring and presentation of didactic information related to the syndrome, the second phase introduced short-term goal contracting concerning the binge eating, and the third phase focused on assertion and relaxation training and on using coping strategies other than binge eating. Results indicated that all patients reduced the frequency of their binge eating-purging episodes. However, due to the small sample size, a statistical analysis of the findings was not conducted. The authors conclude that "short-term group treatment may be a moderately effective treatment intervention for bulimia" (p. 199).

It appears that several authors have found group therapy to be an effective modality for the treatment of bulimia, with most of the group treatment studies mentioned having addressed issues wider than the eating behavior. Some of the groups have been relatively unstructured. Very few of the studies have used a control group, and none of the studies describe a program in detail that can be replicated by other therapists. Similarly, few researchers have used the findings on the characteristics of bulimics in designing their treatment program.

RATIONALE FOR OUR TREATMENT PROGRAM

A review of the literature suggests that although bulimia was once considered a rare disorder (Bruch, 1973), there appears to be an increase in its frequency in both clinical (Stangler & Prinz, 1980) and subclinical (Halmi et al., 1981; Katzman et al., 1984; Pyle et al., 1983) populations. In spite of growing attention to bulimia and its negative consequences, there is very little written on the treatment of this disorder, and as we noted before, existing treatment has focused primarily on the modification of eating habits rather than the personality deficits that may coexist with this disorder.

Despite an awareness of clinical features associated with bulimia as indicated in this review, no treatment program for bulimia has systematically addressed them in its approach. As a result, we decided to develop a treatment program for bulimia based on the previously reported research findings that bulimic women suffer from depression, low self-esteem, poor body image, perfectionist tendencies, and a high need for approval, as well as difficulty in handling negative emotional states such as anger or anxiety, and the setting of unrealistic goals for thinness.

In addition to these research findings, we also incorporated information suggesting that bulimic women need to refine their existing coping styles and to develop competencies. In each session of our 7-week self-enhancement program, a clinical feature found to have been associated with bulimia was addressed. Although we used behavior modification to help the bulimic gain control over her maladaptive eating pattern, most of the attention was on developing new competencies rather than on the binge-purge cycle itself. We designed a treatment packet for each session consisting of reading materials, exercises, and homework for that particular session. It was intended to be used as a workbook and as a self-help guide for maintenance after the termination of the program.

The program includes seven group sessions as well as two additional individual sessions during the course of the group. We have used this program with very encouraging results, finding that relative to no-treatment controls, women who received treatment showed significant improvements in their number of binges per month, self-esteem, and depression (Wolchik, Weiss, & Katzman, in press). Also, the number of purges per month showed a tendency to decrease for the women in the treatment group whereas this behavior increased for women in the no-treatment group. In the 10-week follow-up period, the treatment gains were maintained, with most women continuing to improve during the follow-up period. Our work empirically demonstrated that a short-term psychoeducational approach focusing on personality and behavioral deficits wider than the eating pattern is an effective treatment strategy for bulimia.

Several features of our program deserve attention. First, the presentation of bulimia as a learned habit and the emphasis on building competencies forced the bulimic women to take responsibility for their behavior and instilled hope for change. We would like to emphasize this point, as many of the women who participated in our treatment program were very depressed, a few were suicidal, and some could be described as having long-term character problems. Our emphasis on building positive competencies rather than on pathology helped women make changes in their eating behaviors as well as in how they felt about themselves. Second, the use of a packet containing material similar to that discussed in the therapy session helped to extend the therapeutic value of the sessions and provided material for the clients to refer to following the end of treatment. Also, the group sessions seemed important because they provided opportunities for the women to give each other support and honest feedback and for the women to reduce feelings of isolation and shame. The individual sessions were valuable because they allowed more concentrated focus on each client's unique concerns. Finally, the program is described in detail here and can be used easily by other therapists.

OUTLINE OF THE BOOK

The structure of the book follows the general structure of the group therapy program. Each chapter addresses a particular topic, which is covered during the 7-week program. Chapter 2 discusses the preliminary interview, and Chapters 3–9 describe the topics for each week of the program:

Week 1—Education and overview
Week 2—Eating as coping: developing
    alternative coping strategies
Week 3—Self-esteem, perfectionism, and
    depression
Week 4—Anger and assertiveness
Week 5—Cultural expectations of
    thinness for women
Week 6—Enhancing body image

Week 7—Summing up: where you are now,
   and where do you go from here?

The therapist's role for each week is discussed in each chapter, and at the end of the chapter a summary is provided. Also included at the end of each chapter are homework assignments for that particular week, including handouts for the client. A weekly binge-purge diary is in the appendix. The homework section is addressed to the client. In the homework section, we have sometimes assigned readings from certain books or journals. These materials are easily attainable in libraries and bookstores. However, to spare our clients the cost and inconvenience of attaining this material, we have made copies of the readings for them. We also have loaned them copies of Geneen Roth's book *Feeding the Hungry Heart* (1982) if they did not wish to buy it themselves. We suggest that the therapist using this manual do the same.

The handbook provides practical guidelines, which we have found very useful in working with bulimic women. The program can be used in working with bulimics either individually or in groups. Although we developed it originally for group treatment, it has also been used very successfully with clients treated on an individual basis. There are advantages and disadvantages associated with group and individual treatment, and we do not necessarily endorse one over the other. Practical matters such as time considerations frequently necessitate the use of one mode over another. For this reason, we will discuss issues pertaining to both group and individual treatment. We will primarily describe the group treatment, but modifications can easily be made when working with a client individually.

We will initially review some practical matters such as screening and general format of sessions before discussing treatment. Then we will describe the therapist's role in each session, as well as issues that are likely to come up.

Chapter 2
Preliminary Interview

SCREENING FOR BULIMIA

We see our clients for an initial interview to assess if they are bulimic and to give them some information about the program. We have used the *DSM III* criteria to assess bulimia and to differentiate bulimic women from binge eaters and anorexics.

The diagnostic criteria for bulimia are as follows:

1. Recurrent episodes of binge eating (rapid consumption of a large amount of food in a discrete period of time, usually less than 2 hours).
2. At least three of the following: (a) Consumption of high-caloric, easily ingested food during a binge. (b) Inconspicuous eating during a binge. (c) Termination of such eating episodes by abdominal pain, sleep, social interruption, or self-induced vomiting. (d) Repeated attempts to lose weight by severely restrictive diets, self-induced vomiting, or use of cathartics or diuretics. (e) Frequent weight fluctuations greater than 10 pounds due to alternating binges and fasts.
3. Awareness that the eating pattern is abnormal and fear of not being able to stop voluntarily.
4. Depressed mood and self-deprecating thoughts following eating binges.
5. The bulimic episodes are not due to anorexia nervosa or any known physical disorder.

Even these stringent criteria, however, leave some ambiguity. For example, how much should one eat for it to qualify as a ''binge?'' How frequent should those binges be? What constitutes ''repeated'' attempts to lose weight? For our purposes, we developed operational criteria, which retained the requirements of the *DSM III* (Katzman & Wolchik, 1984), yet quantified them and placed them within a time frame. ''Large quantities of food'' was defined as a minimum of eight binges per month, and

27

"repeated attempts to lose weight" was defined as two or more attempts in the last month. These parameters were chosen to reflect the lower end of the ranges reported in previous studies of bulimia (Mitchell et al., 1981; Pyle et al., 1981). In addition, women could not have been diagnosed as having anorexia nervosa within the last year.

We have used these criteria to define the bulimics included in our treatment studies submitted for publication. We have also included in our groups women whose frequency of binge eating was less than twice a week. However, we have called these women binge-eaters rather than bulimics and have not included their data in our research reports. They seem to have derived some benefit from the group as well.

We have had some problems, however, when we have inadvertently included anorexics in our groups. The dynamics of women with anorexic tendencies are very different from those of bulimics, and the issues of control around food can lead to acting out anorexic tendencies in a group setting and undermining treatment. We have described an example of this situation in another paper (Weiss & Katzman, 1984) in which an anorexic-like woman moved in a diametrically opposite direction from the rest of the group. In a post-group interview with her, she related her "oppositional tendencies," which were reflected in the fact that she abused food as a means of undermining authority. When we included a woman with anorexic tendencies in another group, the control issues were prominent as well, and the woman's "differentness" from the rest of the group was so apparent that it undermined group cohesiveness. However, this woman appeared to benefit from some of the other aspects of the group. We have used parts of this program with a small number of anorexic patients in individual therapy and adapted it to their unique circumstances. In those cases, it was rather successful. It may be that certain aspects of the program can be helpful for women with other eating disorders if used individually rather than in a group setting. However, we have not seen a sufficient number of anorexic women to make any definitive statement. The program was developed specifically for bulimics and based on the research findings on the dynamics of bulimic women, which are clearly different from the dynamics of women with other eating disorders. In view of some of the difficulties we have encountered with anorexic-like women in group settings, it would be important for the therapist to screen out those women from their groups.

It may be difficult to differentiate anorexics and bulimics because of their many similarities and because many bulimics have a history of anorexia. However, there are actually many differences between the two as well. The anorexic woman is at least 25% below normal weight, whereas the bulimic woman is of normal weight. The onset for bulimia, usually in the late teens, is generally later than that for anorexia, which is in the early teens. The anorexic is also less socially and sexually experienced than the bulimic (Pyle et al., 1981). In addition, a disturbed body image is necessary for the diagnosis of anorexia but not for bulimia, according to *DSM III* criteria.

The therapist may be able to screen out women with anorexic tendencies by having them give examples of specific foods consumed in a couple of binges. Frequently, anorexic-like women report "binges." When they are questioned about the amount of food eaten, however, it is determined that the amount does not come close to 1,200 calories. For example, one of the women we inadvertently included in our group listed "five almonds" as a binge in her binge diary. In addition, if the therapist senses much resistance from the client or feels that there may be a power struggle going on, further questioning may be needed before including her in the group.

RECEIVING AND PROVIDING INFORMATION

After ascertaining that the woman fits the operational *DSM III* criteria for bulimia, we attempt to gain a good understanding of her behavior, establish rapport, and introduce her to the group or individual program. A history of the binge-purge behavior is obtained, as well as information on the current binge eating behavior, including the antecedents and functions of the binge. Besides the information on the symptomatic behavior, we obtain a weight history, a family weight history, and a psychiatric

Table 2.1. Intake Form for Bulimics

---

1. Identifying data and referral
   Age: Marital Status: Referral Source:
   Occupation:
2. Current height and weight:
3. Weight history
   Duration of binge eating:
   History of anorexia:
   History of obesity:
4. Psychiatric history (including current treatment):
5. Familial weight history
   Mother: Father: Siblings:
6. Medications:
7. Frequency and caloric intake of binge:
8. Functional analysis (antecedents, where and when, function of binge, consequences):
9. Purging
   Kind used:
   Duration:
   Frequency:
10. Motivation:
11. Fee arrangements:

---

history. A sample brief intake form (Table 2.1), which we usually use, is provided.

After noting the history of past and current binge eating behavior, we describe the treatment to the bulimic woman. We stress several factors when describing the program to a potential member. We state tht the focus of the group is on feelings rather than on eating. Although we deal with eating and nutrition in the group, our emphasis is on helping women find other coping strategies. We discuss how binge eating is frequently used as a way of coping and that in the program we will teach them other ways to deal with stress. We also mention that our program is based on the research findings that bulimic women tend to be depressed, perfectionist, have a low self-esteem, a poor body image, as well as unrealistic expectations of thinness and that each of the sessions focuses on one of these topics. We tell them that the group is a psychoeducational one, with homework assignments after each session.

It is important to provide hope in this and in other sessions by presenting bulimia as a habit that is not beyond one's control and by counteracting some of the popular press coverage that presents it as an "epidemic" that comes upon people suddenly. We stress that the person has control and responsibility for her own treatment. This point cannot be emphasized enough, and we underscore it in our words and actions throughout the program. Bulimic women have tended to see themselves as helpless and out of control. Press reports describing them as "victims" and clinical descriptions of them as "unstable, impulsive personalities," as well as their own negative perceptions of the chronicity and intractibleness of their symptoms, can lead to feelings of despair and hopelessness. The instillment of hope and the taking of responsibility in their own treatment is an essential first step toward making changes.

To convey this feeling of hope and sense of responsibility requires certain attitudinal beliefs on the part of the therapist as well. When we initially interviewed women for our program, we were overwhelmed by the "all-consuming" nature of their behavior. How were we ever going to make any inroads into a habit that appeared to pervade every aspect of their lives? The situation seemed even more overwhelming when we looked at the number of years that many of these women had engaged in this behavior and the extent of depression they felt. Most of the women we saw were clinically depressed, and two were suicidal.[1] In addition, they suffered from low self-esteem and had a poor body image. It is important that the therapist not become discouraged and develop a pessimistic prognosis. A pessimistic attitude only confirms the woman's belief

---

[1] The mean score for our treatment Ss on the Beck Depression Inventory was 18.4, which reflects marked depression.

that she is beyond hope. An overly optimistic attitude on the part of the therapist is not helpful either. Such an attitude can lead to the bulimic's setting unrealistically high goals for change and becoming discouraged. We have tried to encourage bulimics to set realistic goals and not to engage in all-or-nothing thinking. We will elaborate on this approach in a later chapter.

Instilling hope for change goes hand-in-hand with stressing the person's control and responsibility in her own treatment. When the therapist places the responsibility for change in the client's hands, the bulimic begins to realize that she can take charge of her life and begins to develop a sense of her own power. Although the group program is structured and provides direction, we attempt to have the patient do at least 50% of the work in therapy.

In the initial interview, we also outline the structure and format of the program to the bulimic woman. The group is both didactic and experiential, consisting of education, readings, exercises, and discussion in an atmosphere of trust and sharing. The group consists of two co-therapists and a small number of bulimic women, usually from five to seven. It includes seven weekly one-and-a-half-hour sessions as well as a follow-up session 10 weeks after the end of treatment. In addition, each woman has two individual sessions during the course of the group. We included two individual sessions because so much material was ''packed'' into each group session that we wanted to make sure we had a chance to review each woman's unique problems. These sessions are ''booster'' sessions to the group; they do not replace group treatment. One of the individual sessions is scheduled after the second session, and the second one is usually scheduled after the fourth or fifth session.

To encourage commitment and regular group attendance, the fee for the entire program is paid at the beginning of the group. We have found that this usually results in regular attendance. Other leaders of bulimic groups (Roy-Byrne et al., 1984) also suggest a system of monthly payments in advance to ''screen out dilettantes and increase the motivation and commitment to attend for those who sign up'' (p. 14). They reported a relatively high drop-out rate when payment was not required in advance. Because many of our bulimic patients are college students with limited funds, we have generally used a modest fee ($75.00) to cover the eight group and two individual sessions. For individual psychotherapy, fees are set on a sliding scale and paid after each session. Therapists will of course set a fee in line with their own particular setting. We suggest that even under circumstances that do not require payment (e.g., some university counseling or student health centers), clients should make a monetary commitment that will be returned at the end of the program. Regular attendance and a commitment to the program are stressed at the initial interview.

SUMMARY

1. Screen for bulimia, using operational *DMS III* criteria. Binge-eaters who do not strictly fit these criteria in terms of frequency of binge eating (eight times a month) can also benefit from this program, although in our opinion should not be included in any research data about bulimics. Women with anorexic tendencies are not likely to benefit from group treatment and may undermine it.

2. Take a history of binge eating and purging and information on the current behavior. (See Table 2.1.)

3. Present the program to the client: (a) Emphasize feelings and developing coping strategies other than binge eating. (b) Instill hope and emphasize the client's responsibility for her behavior. (c) Describe the structure and format. (d) Set fees so as to encourage regular attendance and commitment to the program.

Chapter 3
Week 1—Education and Overview

GROUP PROCESS

The first session has two purposes: to develop group cohesiveness and to provide an overview of bulimia. When seeing patients individually, we work on establishing rapport rather than on group cohesiveness and may by way of anecdotes bring up some issues if the client does not bring them up herself. Although individual therapy provides greater opportunity to deal with the client's specific problems and allows for more individual attention, the confrontation and feedback from other group members is not available. The interaction among group members is very important, and throughout the program we try to maximize it.

Reasons for Joining the Group

We generally start out the groups by introducing ourselves and having each member tell the group a little about herself and what she would like to take away from the group. To increase cohesiveness, we point out similarities between group members who share common experiences. Women frequently state that their main motivation for starting the program is that they feel out of control, depressed, and guilty about their behavior. "I am so tired of spending my whole life around this. It is time I got on with my life. I don't have the time for this," said Anne, an attractive, intelligent woman in her 20's who had binged and purged for several years before coming to our program. Most women echo this sentiment in one way or another. "I want to feel normal. I don't want to spend the rest of my life thinking about food," said Donna, another young woman in our group.

Feeling abnormal or different was voiced by most women, as well as feeling ashamed of their "secret." Since binge eating and purging are usually secretive behaviors, the feeling of "hiding," of having a major part of their lives hidden, is a significant source of stress for many women. In addition, the financial and medical problems associated with bulimia have prompted some women to come for treatment. Delores, for example, joined our group after she had accumulated $9,000.00 worth of dental bills from all the induced vomiting. In her case, the stomach acid wore away her teeth. Other women mentioned feeling tired, achy, having throat blisters, and any other number of health hazards. Women were also upset by the amount of money that they spent on food, particularly in view of their limited funds. As Donna put it, "How can I explain to my parents where all my money is going to?"

The practical considerations in dealing day by day with bulimia are overwhelming and are only hinted at in the preceding comments. The binge-purge cycle is an all-encompassing symptom and pervades almost every aspect of the bulimic woman's daily existence. She is constantly thinking about food and planning the next binge. This daily preoccupation with food results in deliberate or inadvertent neglect of other areas. The habit interferes with her work, her academic achievement, her social life, and her family relationships.

Because binge eating and purging are secret behaviors, the bulimic woman plans her day around the time when she can be alone in order that she may binge. She may consciously isolate herself from other people so that she can engage in this behavior. She hides her secret from others and withdraws from them, for fear of being "discovered." This isolation and withdrawal further reinforce her feeling that she is "abnormal," "weird" or "different" and prevent her from getting the intimacy she craves.

Not only do her social and family relationships suffer but her functioning in her work or school environment is affected as well. As several of our clients said in one form or another, "It's hard to concentrate on anything else when you are always thinking about food." Jackie, a cute, vivacious bulimic in her late teens who had a nice sense of humor, said, "You know, it can really be dangerous to go out on the road when all that's on your mind is the binge. You're not watching the road or anything else." This preoccupation with food to the exclusion of everything else makes the bulimic neglect other important areas in her life.

Factors other than the preoccupation with food can also lead to neglect of other activities. The depression as well as the fatigue associated with this eating pattern result in limited energy to give to other activities. The bulimic woman may overlook important responsibilities due to the pervading and time consuming nature of her habit.

The financial considerations involved in this behavior are also tremendous. Many bulimic women have limited financial resources; some are students and have no steady income. Because they attempt to hide their behavior from others, as Donna did, it is difficult to explain to their families where their money is going to. They are frequently worried about the monetary aspect of their symptoms. Some women report stealing to support their habit.

The time, energy, and money involved with binge eating and purging make it more than just a daily nuisance. For most women, the behavior is a source of severe stress. Many women report that they are tired of their energies being drained. "We should have better things to do with our time" or "we should be having fun" are comments frequently made.

An additional source of stress lies in the nature of the habit. Because eating is a normal and daily part of living, the bulimic woman is reminded several times at day, at every meal, that she is "different." She cannot let her friends or family see how much she eats; so she avoids going out with them or eating with them. Her hunger resulting from attempts to starve herself is also a constant reminder of her problem. The feelings of depression, shame, isolation, and embarrassment resulting from her "secret" are compounded by the practical concerns.

In addition, the medical and physical problems associated with bulimia add to her stress. Besides the medical and physical hazards of bulimia reported in the literature, there may be many other minor discomforts and symptoms she may feel. However, she does not report these to her doctor because she is embarrassed. For example, most of the women we saw reported menstrual irregularities, yet not one of them mentioned these to her gynecologist for fear of divulging her secret. Many bulimics have an underlying anxiety about their health but are afraid to say anything about it lest others find out about their habit.

Emphasis on Feelings

We encourage the discussion of feelings rather than of food intake or purging methods. We view bulimia as an eating disorder associated with personality and behavioral variables, and we focus on the feeling and coping aspects of behavior rather than on the eating and vomiting. This is clearly a reversal of what the women have done before. Because much of their energy and thoughts revolve around food, we do not wish to reinforce such thinking. Instead, we attempt to teach them other ways of coping. In addition, we want to avoid some of the possible unfortunate byproducts of learning different methods of purging that can occur in groups of this sort.

To help them talk freely, we let them know that everything said in the group is confidential, that they are free to discuss their issues with others, but are not free to talk about other group members. We help women discuss their feelings of shame, disgust, guilt, anger, and hurt about their behavior. The ability to share these feelings, sometimes for the first time, helps them realize that they are not alone and provides them with support and understanding from others. It is also a relief finally to be able to express their feelings and be understood. Many women feel that nobody can really understand the behavior about which they feel so disgusted. "I tell my friends that I binge but I don't think anyone really understands what I mean by that or knows how much I eat," said Jackie. "I get so disgusted with myself. I would die if anyone ever found out," she added. Other women reported trying so hard to be "good" but being unable to stop the binge eating. "Every day I tell myself it will never happen again, but then I do it and I feel more and more out of control" said Anne. Others frequently nod in understanding and are relieved finally to be able to talk about their "terrible secret."

Besides helping women express feelings of shame, guilt, and disgust about their behavior, the therapist can look for and encourage expression of anger about their dilemma. Women frequently report anger and frustration about social pressures to be thin. As Anne put it, "Every time you read a magazine, you see these delicious gourmet recipes on the one hand and then you see these skinny models on the other, and you feel you're getting two messages." Women are angry that they do not fit the model-slim image and that they are not able to eat what they want. The feelings of deprivation, frustration, and anger are prominent.

Not every group member has to express these feelings in order to deal with them. Group members can share in others' experiences, and as one woman works out her feelings, others can empathize and relate it to their own. As one member discusses her feelings, the others may merely listen and share vicariously; yet they benefit from it. One woman can provide an experience that the rest of the group members can benefit from vicariously.

Hope

It is important that these feelings of shame, guilt, disgust, and anger are dealt with so that women can get beyond the feelings of shame to a sense of mutuality and hope. Hope is an integral part of the program, and this is provided throughout by stressing each woman's ability to take charge of her life. Many women also experience hope as they see others changing their eating habits. As Celia, a woman in our group, said after watching some women make changes, "If they can do it, so can I."

However, it is also important to set realistic expectations for change. In view of the bulimic's perfectionist tendencies, she may set unrealistically high goals for change and become discouraged and depressed, reverting to old patterns. We encourage women to set realistic goals for change and tell them not to set the goals of elimination of binge eating and purging by the end of treatment, but rather strive to decrease the frequency of these behaviors.

Group Cohesiveness

Much of this session is devoted to helping group members develop a sense of cohesiveness while providing educational information. We attempt to integrate the experiences of group members with the educational material and to use their experiences as a springboard for discussion. A blackboard or flipchart and group discussion make this procedure personal and informal. A flipchart can be more effective than writing on the blackboard because members can refer back to what was said in previous sessions. We usually ask questions and let group members provide the answers rather than lecture to them.

The development of group cohesiveness is very important, and we try to maximize interaction between members as much as possible. According to Yalom, "members of cohesive groups are more accepting of each other, more supportive, more inclined to form meaningful relationships in the group" (1970, p. 56). Berzon, Pious, and Parson (1963) showed that the main curative mechanism of their short-term therapy was the interaction among group members. Throughout the program, we encourage group members to relate to each other. As one member talks, we may ask others to respond to her or to give their reactions to what she is saying. We frequently ask if others have had the same experience or share similar feelings.

Many factors of the group process make it helpful for the bulimic woman. As she enters a group with women like herself, she feels less isolated and less abnormal. The experience of sharing negative feelings and still being accepted by other group members helps free her from these feelings. The group also provides her with the support she needs in order to make changes. The support comes from knowing that others are coping with the same feelings and fears that she is. Group members can be confrontative as well as supportive and put pressure on a woman to make changes. It is more difficult to resist pressure from women like herself than from a therapist who may "not understand what it's like." The group also provides each woman an opportunity for learning through others' experiences and increases her feelings of competency and self-esteem through helping others. As noted before, the sense of hope while watching others make changes can be a major motivator in helping the bulimic woman take the necessary steps for change as well.

The group process may be especially effective for bulimic women given their difficulties in interpersonal relationships. Loro and Orleans (1981) have suggested that bulimics are underassertive and have interpersonal problems. Hawkins' (1982) findings that bulimics may have difficulty expressing themselves directly and have a pattern representative of an overt or passive-aggressive demanding attitude and Johnson et al.'s (1983) findings that bulimics score higher than normals on interpersonal sensitivity support this contention. The group can help women express themselves more directly and receive feedback on their interpersonal style from others.

Furthermore, an all-female group is effective in reversing some of the stereotypic female sex-role behavior that is hypothesized to be a central component of bulimia (Boskind-White & White, 1983). In this group, the bulimic woman does not look to male authority figures for direction but focuses on the strengths within herself. In addition, she learns to value the support and friendship of other females. We address this issue in more detail in chapter 7. In that session, we help women develop insight into their behavior around male and towards female friends.

PROVIDING AN OVERVIEW
OF BULIMIA

Definition, Advantages,
and Disadvantages

Following the introductions and discussion of feelings, we provide some basic information on bulimia—what it is and what it is not. Much of the information we provide is included at the end of this chapter (see p. 42). We discuss some of the psychological and health hazards of bulimia, many of which the group members have already mentioned by now as they have talked about themselves. The psychological problems associated with bulimia are the depression, withdrawal, anxiety, guilt, and shame that they understand too well. Some bulimics may already be experiencing some of the physical complications of bulimia, which include rotting teeth, electrolyte imbalance, throat blisters, anemia, ruptured stomach and esophagus, as well as other problems. The potential health hazards are eye-openers to some women, and there can be a profound effect on the group if a group member is already experiencing some medical problems. We give this information matter-of-factly, not so much to scare them and add to their depression, but to point out some of the adverse effects of their behavior. It is important not to make bulimia glamorous, as many bulimics still feel it's the easiest way of dieting. We stress that bulimia is not having one's cake and eating it too, as many people think.

Myths and Misconceptions

We also attempt to clarify some of the myths and misconceptions about bulimia. We encourage discussion by asking, "What have you heard about bulimia?" or "What do other people think it is?" We dispute some of the popular myths and misconceptions about bulimia: that it is chronic, that it is incurable, that it is beyond one's control, or that it is a mental illness, among other misconceptions.

When we ask women what they had heard about bulimia, there is generally embarrassed laughter before they volunteer that being bulimic means you are "crazy," "abnormal," or "mentally ill." Although the term bulimia is listed by the American Psychiatric Association as a diagnostic entity, a woman who fits this description is no more "crazy" than a woman who shows symptoms of depression. Labeling this behavior a mental illness can have serious implications for treatment because the bulimic feels that this behavior is outside her control. We present bulimia as a habit, one that can be unlearned just as it was learned.

A second misconception about bulimia is that the bulimic woman has no control when she is around food and that she is taken over by an "uncontrollable urge." This myth also takes the responsibility away from the woman. In truth, the bulimic woman has a great deal of control over her behavior. Frequently, much planning is needed to set the scene for a binge to occur. Bulimics frequently plan their binges at a time when they are alone. Many won't binge when they are on a trip or in a situation where they are around others.

Other irrational beliefs about bulimia have kept women from seeking help or changing their behavior. The popular press has generally depicted bulimia as being chronic and intractible, taking years to develop and years to eliminate. As Penny, an attractive and verbal woman, stated on the first session, "I have not heard or read of any bulimic woman who got better." This creates pessimism and a "what's the use?" feeling. The truth is that women with a long history of binge eating and purging have made changes. It is important for the therapist to mention this, as it provides hope for members and encourages them to try new coping responses.

Another misconception that may prevent women from changing their eating behavior is that if they stop binge eating and purging, they will have to change in other ways as well. Many women blame their eating habits for everything that is going wrong in their lives and are afraid to find out that their lives will not change if they stop binge eating. Celia expressed it like this: "As long as I binge, nothing much is really expected of me. I mean, really, what can you expect from someone who has so little control over her life? Having this habit keeps me from going out with others, keeps me broke, gives me a good excuse not to do well in school. . . . "

The therapist needs to detach the binge eating from any of the emotional connotations the woman assigns to it by reassuring her that giving up the habit means giving up binge eating and purging, nothing more. In dispelling the myths, we provide a sense of responsibility and control for the bulimic over her own behavior. This gives her hope and also helps her from "copping out" by disclaiming responsibility for her eating patterns.

Cop-outs

We ask group members what other types of cop-outs they use that are primarily related to abdicating control over their behavior. We write these on the board and show them the list (see Figure 3.1). Group members frequently smile when they read the list of cop-out statements, as they have been using these themselves. Awareness of their cop-outs helps them gain more control over their behavior, and they are less likely to use these as excuses for binge eating in future group sessions. We have each woman tell us what her cop-outs would be, and encourage group members to call on each others' cop-outs. This promotes group interaction and lets group members rather than therapists confront a woman who is copping out. A common cop-out is for a group member to skip a session, particularly if she has done well or conversely, if she has had a bad week. We stress the importance of regular attendance to the meetings.

FIGURE 3.1. Common Cop-outs

I've been doing this for so long I can't change.
Something just overtakes me.
It's a habit.
I don't even realize I'm doing it.
I can't lose weight any other way.
Once I start I can't stop.
This has been such a stressful week.
I can't give up my laxatives yet.
I can keep the laxatives, I just won't use them.
I don't even try to throw up, it just happens.

Which of These Do You Use?

What Are Some Other Cop-Outs?

Women who use laxatives to maintain their weight may cop-out by saying they will keep the laxatives in their purse ("I just won't use them") or "I'm not ready to throw out my laxatives yet." These women are really saying, "I want to continue binge eating and purging but I won't take the responsibility for that by saying it out loud." We inform the laxative users that an essential component of the program is throwing away the laxatives by the second week.

At the end of this session, we also give a brief preview of the next six sessions and outline the topics we will be covering for the next 6 weeks. For homework, we ask them to review the material on bulimia and to start filling out the binge diary (see Appendix for sample form). We tell them that we know this will be difficult to do but that they need to look at what is happening with them prior to a binge so that they can change it. We emphasize that before they can change their eating habits, they need to see exactly what they are thinking and feeling before a binge in order to develop alternative coping responses. The usefulness of the binge diary is underscored. We ask them to record only binges, not each meal. We caution that a binge has to be at least 1,200 calories and that it should not be a meal. Many women have a tendency to write down any oversized portion or snack as a binge. We also ask them to note the number of purges. We encourage them to write down exactly what they were thinking and feeling before the binge.

SUMMARY

1. Have group members introduce themselves and state their goals for the group. Help them set realistic goals for change.
2. Develop group cohesiveness by letting group members talk about their shame, anger, guilt, and other feelings about their problem.
3. Provide an overview of bulimia including basic information, psychological and physical hazards, myths, and cop-outs.
4. Describe the program, with its emphasis on feelings rather than on food intake, and provide a brief overview of the coming sessions.
5. Give members homework for the 1st week.

HOMEWORK

1. Read "Bulimic Basics" at the end of the chapter and "The Gorging-Purging Syndrome" by Marlene Boskind-Lodhal and Joyce Sirlin (*Psychology Today*, 1977, March). (If you want, also start reading *Feeding the Hungry Heart* by Geneen Roth, New York: Bobbs-Merrill Co., 1982).
2. Review the list of cop-outs (Figure 3.1) and circle the ones you use. Add additional ones, and refer to these from time to time.

3. Start recording your binges in the binge-purge diary (see Appendix) for Week 1. Record only the *binges* for that week and not everything you eat. A binge has to be at least 1,200 calories, and it should not be a meal. Do not include oversized portions or regular snacks as binges. Write down everything you ate during the binge, and your thoughts and feelings prior to eating. You don't need to fill out the alternative coping responses yet until the next session, unless you can note some specific things you could have done instead of binge eating. Please record the total number of binges and purges for this week in the diary.

BULIMIC BASICS
What Is Bulimia?

Bulimia is a name that describes a combination of thoughts and actions. These include:

1. Eating large quantities of food in short periods of time (binge eating).
2. Vomiting, exercising, or fasting after a binge.
3. Repeated attempts to lose weight and frequent fluctuations in weight.
4. Binge eating in private, stopping when someone comes home.
5. Eating foods that are high in calories and require little preparation.
6. Feeling bad about yourself after a binge.
7. Feeling depressed about your eating habits.

Who Is Bulimic?

Bulimia occurs most often in college-aged women. Women who are perfectionist about their bodies and their lives (high achievers) often begin this cycle at about age 18.

How Many Women Are Bulimic?

Approximately 4% of college women demonstrate bulimic behaviors.

What Are the Advantages of the Binge-Purge Cycle?

On the surface, it appears that you can have your cake and eat it too. People think it is an "easy" way to eat and stay slim.

What Are the Disadvantages of Bulimia?

Bulimia has both psychological and physical disadvantages. The bulimic feels out of control, guilty, depressed, embarrassed, alone, and her secret limits her social contacts. Although she originally engages in this behavior to become attractive, this may result in very unattractive physical changes such as rotting teeth, stomach ruptures, and other medical complications. In addition, the stench from the vomiting can be repulsive to the bulimic and those around her.

What Can Be Done About It?

As bulimics are coming out of the closet, more and more programs are being developed to meet their needs. Counseling, addressing both psychological issues and eating behavior, can help the woman gain control of her life and eating habits.

Chapter 4

Week 2—Eating as Coping: Developing Alternative Coping Strategies

CUES FOR BINGE EATING

This is an important week in treatment because we cover much material that sets the stage for later sessions. In chapter 1 we reviewed the research findings and theoretical models that suggest that bulimic women have limited coping abilities and that binge eating is an ineffective and self-defeating coping response for most bulimics. The purpose of this session is to help women identify the cues that lead to binge eating for them and to develop other responses to these cues. We attempt to identify a woman's cues for binge eating by reviewing her binge diary at the beginning of the session. The cues are usually threefold: her feelings, her thoughts, and her excessive hunger due to starvation. After identifying these three types of cues for binge eating, we spend the rest of the session discussing alternative ways of coping. We discuss ways to deal with feelings more directly, to change self-defeating thoughts, and to develop better eating habits.

We start the session by reviewing the binge diaries and asking the women to tell us their thoughts and feelings prior to binge eating. This is frequently difficult for them to do, but with time they become better at identifying their thoughts and feelings. Eating for most of the women is a means of coping with stress. Some common emotional triggers for binge eating are boredom, loneliness, anger, and anxiety. Connie is typical of many women. She told the group, ''It seems I eat just because I'm home alone. I don't even think about it. It's automatic. I go home, I'm alone, and that's a cue for me to eat. Whether it's boredom, loneliness, or habit

I don't know." Other women binge while studying, "I think of all the work I have to do," said Celia, "and then all I think about is food. I feel so nervous." "This has been such a stressful week, so I eat just to relax and forget about it," said another. Some women binge when they look at other women and feel "fat" by comparison. Others eat as a means of avoiding difficult situations; still others eat when they are feeling angry.

Excessive hunger is also a trigger for binge eating. Ironically, the only time women eat out of hunger is when this hunger is excessive and caused by near starvation. A woman binges after being "good" all day and not giving the body what it needs. Many women do not feed their bodies because they do not realize how much they can eat and not gain weight. They feel the least bit of food intake will result in immediate weight gain. In addition, the bulimic woman has no idea what her ideal weight is, and she strives to weigh less than she should according to her height and bone structure.

Thoughts also serve as cues for binge eating, and we help women identify what they are thinking. Frequently, these thoughts include statements such as, "I'm so nervous, I have to eat," or "Since I'm going to purge anyway, I might as well eat the whole thing," or "I'm going on a diet tomorrow, this is my last chance to eat."

ALTERNATIVE COPING
RESPONSES

Changing Eating Habits

After helping women identify their cues for binge eating, we teach them alternative ways of coping. For example, a woman who eats after talking to her mother is encouraged to express her feelings about the conversation directly. A woman who eats out of boredom can take a walk, go to a movie, or read the paper. A woman who eats to console herself can ask for comfort from friends. In addition, some specific strategies can help many women change their cues for eating. For example, a woman who eats when she is home alone studying can study at the library. Another woman who has an "uncontrollable urge" to eat can set a timer for 20 minutes and during this time polish her nails, vacuum, call a friend, or keep busy in a number of ways. Other strategies for confronting a binge can be suggested by the group members.

Although the main focus of the treatment program is on feelings rather than on food, we present some basic nutritional information because an insufficient familiarity with nutrition leads many women to binge. Learning good eating habits is one of the basic coping skills. We ask each woman to look at her recommended weight from the Metropolitan Height and

Weight Table for Women (1983) because most set their ideal weight at least 10 or 20 pounds below these norms (see Table 4.1). We challenge the notion that every woman should weigh 103 lb and stress that they are trying to achieve unrealistic goals that are neither ideal nor healthy. Most women are surprised by this table and are reluctant at first to accept that they may already be within their weight range or lower. Some, however, realize that they may be putting excessive pressure on themselves to be thin, and that trying to live up to some unrealistic image of slimness only results in frustration and depression.

We also provide some basic information on how much they can eat and still maintain their weight. We review some of "Fat Facts" listed in Table 4.2 and encourage them to eat healthy and regular meals. In this session, we review a typical menu consisting of 1,320 and 1,488 calories daily needed to maintain weights of 110 lb and 124 lb, respectively, and demonstrate that women can eat three healthy meals and still maintain their weights. A menu for 1,320 calories is listed in Table 4.2 and other menus for 1,488 calories are listed in Table 4.3. We tell them not to weigh themselves daily and to use exercise rather than starvation to reduce. Many women are skeptical that they can eat so "much" and still maintain their weight, and they are frequently surprised that they do not become obese overnight by developing healthy eating habits.

We stress the importance of eating three meals a day because starvation and its accompanying feelings of deprivation invariably lead to binge eat-

Table 4.1. 1983 Metropolitan Height and Weight Table*

HEIGHT FEET/INCHES	SMALL FRAME	MEDIUM FRAME	LARGE FRAME
4 10	102–111	109–121	118–131
4 11	103–113	111–123	120–134
5 0	104–115	113–126	122–137
5 1	106–118	115–129	125–140
5 2	108–121	118–132	128–143
5 3	111–124	121–135	131–147
5 4	114–127	124–138	134–151
5 5	117–130	127–141	137–155
5 6	120–133	130–144	140–159
5 7	123–136	133–147	143–163
5 8	126–139	136–150	146–167
5 9	129–142	139–153	149–170
5 10	132–145	142–156	152–173
5 11	135–148	145–159	155–176
6 0	138–151	148–162	158–179

*Metropolitan Life Insurance Company, Health and Safety Education Division.

Table 4.2. Fat Facts

How many calories can I eat and still maintain my weight?
Multiply your current weight by 12—that's how many calories you can eat and not gain weight. For example: You weigh 110 lb: 110×12=1,320. So, you can eat 1,320 calories a day and still maintain your weight.

About how much food is that?
1,320 Calories = 1 egg, 1 english muffin with jam, orange juice, turkey sandwich with cheese and mayonnaise, potato chips, 4 oz chicken, baked potato, salad, vegetable, apple. 1,320 Calories = 2 bags of M & M's, 5 chocolate chip cookies, dish of ice cream, 1 piece of pie. You can eat all of this and still maintain your weight!

What is a healthy weight for a person of my height and frame?
Use Table 4.1 to find the range of weight that has been shown to be associated with lowest mortality for women of your height and frame. The weights include indoor clothing weighing about 3 lb. The heights include 1 inch for heels.

How many calories can I eat and still lose 1 lb a week? Two pounds?
One pound of fat is equal to 3,200 calories. Reduce your intake by 3,200 and you lose a pound. Reduce intake by 450 calories a day and lose 1 lb a week. Reduce intake by 900 calories a day and lose 2 lb a week. So, if you want to weigh 110 lb, you can eat 870 calories a day and still lose 1 lb a week as you head toward your goal.

What if I want to lose weight faster?
Increasing your activity level means that your body needs more calories to maintain your weight. Increasing activity without increasing eating means you will lose weight faster. Regular exercise helps you reduce and stay slim.

How do I know if I'm looking slimmer?
Getting on the scale daily is not helpful. What you weigh on a particular day is not necessarily an indicator of weight gain or weight loss. At times, especially before your period and midway through your cycle, water retention may be the cause for your weight to go up. Also, inches lost through exercise may not be reflected on the scale. Remember, muscle weighs more than fat.

---

ing. We state that starvation can lead to an increased interest and preoccupation with food, and bulimia can be a natural physiological consequence. We tell them that, in the long run, they lose weight much faster by developing a regular pattern. Many women resist this because they are afraid that they will gain weight overnight if they eat three meals a day. We generally deal with the fears by asking them to try it for 1 week. After all, we point out, they are in the program to change their eating habits. We ask them to experiment by eating regularly for a week and seeing what happens.

We also ask them to make up their minds, at least for this week, not to purge after a binge, *no matter how much they have eaten*. If they generally vomit after a large meal, they may be using purging as an excuse to continue eating. They may say to themselves, ''I might as well overeat since

I am going to throw up afterwards." Many women cut down on the size of their binges once they know they are not going to get rid of the food. We tell laxative abusers to throw out their laxatives after this session, as a commitment not to purge. We also give them some reading material that describes research findings on laxative use. These findings indicate that laxative use still results in 88% caloric absorption of the food, so laxatives are not an effective mechanism for losing weight (Bo-Linn, Santa Ana, Morawski, & Fordtran, 1983). It should be noted that very few of the women we saw used laxatives heavily or as the primary mode of purging.

Table 4.3. Typical Menus for 1,488 Calories*

BREAKFAST	LUNCH	DINNER
Fried Egg	Tuna Sandwich	Fried Pork Chop
2 Strips Bacon	10 French Fries	½ c Applesauce
1 Slice Toast	Apple	Salad with Dressing
		½ c Rice
		1,470
Bagel	B.L.T.	Chicken Breast—Broiled
Cream Cheese	10 Potato Chips	½ c Noodles with Butter
	Tangerine	Broccoli with Butter
		Apple
		1,430
English Muffin	Roast Beef Sandwich	Sirloin Steak—Broiled
Jelly	Salad with Dressing	Baked Potato
Orange Juice	Orange	Green Beans with Butter
		½ Cantalope
		1,480
Fried Egg	Fruit-Flavored Yogurt	Fried Scallops
English Muffin	Apple	Rice with Butter
Jelly		Salad with Dressing
Orange Juice		
		1,450
Apple Pie		
2 Doughnuts		
Chocolate Ice Cream		
Sundae		
Cheesecake		
1,450		
Candy Bar		
Chocolate Cake		
Eclair		
3 Chocolate Chip Cookies		
1,440		
2 Jelly Doughnuts		
2 Scoops Ice Cream		
4 Fig Newtons		
2 Brownies		
1,400		

*Height: 5'4"; Weight: 124 lb; Frame: Medium; Calories/day to maintain at 124 lb = 1,488.

With heavy laxative users, referral to a physician for supervised tapering of laxatives is recommended. Because the main motivation for taking laxatives is to lose weight, clear demonstration of their ineffectiveness as a means of weight control generally results in discontinuing this practice. Compliance is also influenced by group pressure and the emphasis on taking responsibility for one's behavior.

I Cope

In addition to developing new eating habits as a coping response, we review some other coping skills to help the bulimic deal with feelings of stress prior to binge eating. The acronym *I COPE*[1] stands for some basic coping skills and contains ideas for stress management (see Table 4.4). In this acronym, *I* stands for Identifying stress, and each of the letters in the word *COPE* stands for a different stress skill: Communication, Organ-

Table 4.4. ''I COPE'': Identifying stress, Communication, Organization, Perception, Enhancement.

IDENTIFYING STRESS
How do you know when you are experiencing stress?

COMMUNICATION SKILLS
Becoming Assertive: Expressing your needs and saying ''no.''
Listening: Listening to the feelings of others.
Making Contact: Finding friends who listen to you and support you.
Which of these skills can you use the most?

ORGANIZATIONAL SKILLS
Pacing: Choosing the rhythm that works for you.
Setting Priorities: Deciding how you spend your time.
Planning: Setting goals and working toward them.
Which of these skills can you use the most?

PERCEPTION SKILLS
Relabeling: Changing the way you think about some things.
Letting Go: Accepting what you cannot change.
Whispering: Giving yourself gentle, positive messages.
Which of these skills can you use the most?

ENHANCEMENT SKILLS
Taking Care of Your Body: Eating, sleeping, and exercising properly.
Gentleness: Treating yourself kindly and gently.
Relaxing: Taking time to relax through breathing, meditation, and other ways.
Which of these skills can you use the most?

---

[1] Acronym developed by the authors. The stress skills are adapted from Donald Tubesing's Stress Skills Workshop presented in Phoenix, AZ, 1978.

ization, Perception, and Enhancement. We give an example of how this acronym can be applied to binge eating. A woman heading for the refrigerator as she is studying for a test can first *identify* her feelings. She may be feeling anxious, tired, or bored. She can then use one of the coping skills to deal with her stress. She can call a friend and discuss her feelings (*communication*), organize her material and feel more prepared (*organization*), see the test as a small part of her education rather than a monumental task (*perception*), or exercise, relax, or nap to feel renewed (*enhancement*). After discussing the *I COPE* skills we ask each woman which of the skills will help her most.

Changing Thought Patterns

We also discuss the effect that our thinking has on our eating behavior and illustrate how women's negative monologues encourage binge eating. We provide examples from Table 4.5 and discuss how we can replace our negative monologues with more appropriate ones. This is similar to some of the methods described by Garner and Bemis (1982) in their work with anorexics. We try to elicit each woman's negative monologues and have her replace them with more positive ones. In each of the succeeding sessions, we discuss the negative thoughts women are "feeding" themselves as we review their binge diaries with them.

Many of the negative thoughts are typical of the overgeneralization and all-or-nothing thinking in which bulimics frequently engage. For example, Anne told herself, "If I gain 1 lb, I will go on and gain 20." We challenged the irrationality behind the thought by asking, "Why should you necessarily gain 20 lb if you gain a pound?" and asked her to replace her negative monologue with a more appropriate one. Another example of overgeneralization is when a women tells herself, as Jackie did, "I blew it! I ate one cookie, and there goes my diet!" She can replace this with a more appropriate monologue such as "Why should one cookie blow it for me?"

We also challenge the notion that binge eating and purging are successful weight control methods. For example, Delores told herself, "I've discovered an easy way to diet." She was encouraged to change her thinking to "This is an easy way to die! I can lose my teeth, rupture my stomach, and hurt my kidneys." The notion that one can become attractive by purging to stay slim is also attacked. For example, Jackie told herself, "I'm going to vomit until I'm thin and pretty." We confronted her with the more realistic and unattractive thought that "Continuous vomiting will make my teeth fall out—that's not very attractive." That thinness will automatically result in popularity with the opposite sex is also challenged, as in Penny's case. Penny told herself, "If I'm thin and beautiful, then my boy-

Table 4.5. Changing the Way You Think

NEGATIVE MONOLOGUES	APPROPRIATE MONOLOGUES
"I want to lose weight fast."	"I'll gain the weight right back if I don't change my eating habits."
"If I gain 1 pound, I'll go on and gain 20 pounds."	"This is crazy all-or-nothing thinking."
"Gaining 10 lb would push me over the edge."	"There I go again with my crazy thinking."
"I've discovered an easy way to diet. I can eat everything and not have to count calories."	"This is an easy way to die! My teeth will fall out, my stomach will rupture, and my esophagus will get inflamed."
"Eating sweets is the only way to give myself a real treat. It's the one way that I know to cheer myself up."	"I can use the time I spend binge eating and throwing up to have fun in other ways."
"The only way to relax while studying is to nibble."	"There are other ways to relax. Why not call a friend or take a walk?"
"I had a ghastly day. I think I'll cheer myself up with a snack."	"Think how terrible I will feel afterwards."
"I was good all day. I will just have a little pick now."	"There's no such thing as a 'little pick' when my stomach is empty. Next time I won't starve myself—that's not being good!"
"I don't feel like doing anything at the moment. I'll make something to eat."	"I'm really not hungry. Binge eating will make me feel bad afterwards. Why don't I do something else instead?"
"I'm so tense. If I eat this bag of cookies and throw up, I'll feel better."	"Nonsense. Vomiting makes me feel gross. There are other ways to relax."
"I'm all alone now. It's my chance to eat."	"Nonsense. This is not the only time to eat. If I eat sensibly, I could enjoy my meals with others."
"It's there. It's free. Why let it go to waste?"	"I'm going to throw it up anyway. Why bother going through the trouble of eating and vomiting?"
"I blew it with that doughnut. There goes my diet."	"Why should one sweet blow it for me?"
"If I eat a candy it will instantly be converted into stomach fat."	"No one gets fat from one sweet."
"If I eat one cookie, I'll have to eat the whole box."	"I can enjoy one cookie, but eating the whole box won't make me feel any better."

(continued)

Table 4.5. Changing the Way You Think (*continued*)

NEGATIVE MONOLOGUES	APPROPRIATE MONOLOGUES
"I just can't control myself."	"Of course I can control myself. I control myself too much."
"Eating is the only way I can feel in control."	"Nonsense! Look how many problems it has caused already. This is crazy thinking again."
"Eating is disgusting. Now I feel like a cow."	"Eating is natural. If I eat naturally, I don't have to feel like a cow."
"If I can't control my eating, I'm not worth anything."	"I am more than my eating habits."
"I have this gross bulge in my stomach. I better vomit it off."	"Vomit is more gross. Everyone's stomach extends after eating. Let the food digest and the bulge will disappear."
"I'm going to vomit until I'm thin and pretty."	"Continuous vomiting will make my teeth fall out—that's not very attractive."
"If I'm thin and beautiful then my boyfriend will want to be with me more."	"I'm always so worried that he'll discover 'my secret.' I don't even let myself enjoy the time with him. I should just be myself."
"I can't stop thinking about sweets."	"Whenever I find myself thinking about food, I can change the topic to some other pleasant experience."
"I just want to taste, no need to cut off a portion."	"When I eat standing in front of the refrigerator I can't tell how much I'm eating. I'll just cut myself a piece, sit down, and enjoy it."

friend will want to spend more time with me." She learned to remind herself of the reality of her situation and change her monologue to "I'm always so worried that he'll discover 'my secret,' I don't even let myself enjoy the time with him."

The self-defeating rather than the reinforcing qualities of binges are also emphasized when changing negative monologues to more appropriate ones. For example, Connie frequently told herself, "I had a terrible day. I'll cheer myself up with food afterwards." She changed her thinking to "Think how terrible I will feel afterwards." Similarly, a woman who thinks "I am so nervous I have to eat," can remind herself that "Binge eating creates psychological problems—it doesn't get rid of them." In addition, other coping strategies are usually suggested in the new monologues. For example, a woman who tells herself she needs to binge because she is bored or tense can remind herself, "There are other ways to relax. Why not take a walk?"

After we discuss all the different coping responses, we ask each woman to focus on one new coping response for the following week. We enlist the aid of the group in generating some coping strategies for each woman. Sometimes, we make photocopies of the different coping responses developed by the group members and hand them out to each member at the next session.

This is a "packed" session, and we attempt to cover a great deal of material. Obviously we will not be able to have each woman identify all of her triggers for binge eating and change her eating habits in one session. This session, however, lays the groundwork for future sessions, and we frequently repeat over and over the basic information provided here. This is a good time to schedule an individual session with each woman if she is part of a group, so that we can review her pattern in detail.

We also collect the binge diaries at this (and every) session so we can ensure that the women are filling them out properly, and we give them written feedback. Reviewing the diary is important for the therapist in understanding exactly what happens with each woman. In addition, it underscores for the client the importance of filling the diary out. If women "forget" or "do not want to write down" everything, we discuss the feelings behind the "forgetting."

For homework, we ask each group member to review the material on alternative ways to cope with stress and on nutrition and to develop her own list of coping responses. As noted before, we encourage her very strongly to eat three meals a day and to make a decision not to purge even if she binges. As she continues filling out the binge diary, we ask her to write in the third column alternative coping responses she can use the next time she is in a similar situation.

SUMMARY

1. Go over the homework, and help each woman identify her thoughts and feelings prior to binge eating. Write on the board the triggers for binge eating, which are usually feelings, thoughts, and excessive hunger due to starvation.
2. Review "Fat Facts" (Table 4.2) and demonstrate how much the women can eat and still maintain their weight. Encourage them to eat three meals daily and to make up their minds not to purge this week regardless of the size of their binge. Tell laxative users to throw their laxatives away.
3. Discuss alternative ways of coping other than binge eating. Review and

demonstrate the "I COPE" concept (Table 4.4) and "Changing the Way You Think" (Table 4.5).

4. Help each woman identify her own alternate coping responses.
5. Collect the binge diaries and give the homework for the following week. Schedule an individual session with each woman if you are doing group treatment.

HOMEWORK

1. Review the materials, including "Fat Facts," "I COPE," and "Changing the Way You Think" (Tables 4.2, 4.4, and 4.5).
2. Develop your own list of alternative coping behaviors and write them down.
3. Continue filling out the binge diary (see Appendix). This time fill out all three columns. If you do binge this week, write down what else you could have done so that you can use that the next time you are in a similar situation.

Chapter 5
Week 3—Self-Esteem, Perfectionism, and Depression

In the first chapter, we reviewed literature that indicated that in comparison with both binge eaters and controls, bulimics were more depressed, had lower self-esteem, and had higher self-expectations (Katzman & Wolchik, 1984). We also reviewed some of the research findings supporting the relationship between bulimia and depression. Our clinical observations of bulimics were consistent with the empirical studies. Many of the women we saw were clinically depressed, and a few were suicidal. As we noted in the footnote in the second chapter, the mean score for our treatment subjects on the Beck Depression Inventory was 18.4, which is suggestive of marked depression.

In this session, we elicit a discussion on the relationship between depression, self-esteem, and perfectionism and how they apply to both personal and weight goals. Afterwards, women participate in three exercises. The first helps them become aware of the stringent demands they place on themselves. The second helps them to learn to nourish themselves in ways that do not require food. The third exercise helps them to raise their self-esteem.

PERFECTIONISM AND BULIMIA

We use David Burns' article, ''The Perfectionists Script for Self-Defeat,'' *Psychology Today* (1980, November) as a springboard for discussion. This article reviews the pitfalls of setting extremely high standards for oneself and describes some of the unpleasant consequences of perfectionist behavior. Contrary to popular thought, the setting of unrealistic goals leads to poorer performance. It also frequently results in depression, low self-esteem, and other negative psychological states. The thought and behavior patterns of perfectionists are described well in this article. We begin by asking group members what they think perfectionism is. After some talk among them, we define it as not so much as trying to do an excellent job but as setting impossible and unrealistic goals. When goals are set so high, nothing is ever good enough. Group members give examples of how they set unrealistic goals for themselves—both weight and personal goals. When we ask, "What is thin enough for you? At what point will you look at yourself and say this is the right weight for me?" most women reply "Never." Even when they do have a weight goal in mind, usually 100 or 105 lb, it is usually unrealistic and based on an arbitrary number. When we ask them what they think will happen when they reach their desired weights, they typically respond that they would probably strive for an even lower weight. For many bulimics, one can never be thin enough. We integrate this with the previous week's discussion of how so many women set their goals way below the standards suggested by the Metropolitan Life Insurance Company.

Many of our women had such high expectations in areas other than weight (e.g., getting straight A's, studying every spare minute, and so on) that many were defeated before they started. Group members gave examples of how they measured their worth by their success and productivity and felt depressed when they were unable to attain their goals. We review research findings that suggest perfectionists are more likely to be depressed (Burns, 1980) and ask group members why they think that perfectionism leads to depression. Many give examples of how they tend to perceive themselves as failures and as inadequate when they fail to reach their goals.

Anne is an example of many bulimic women in the goals she set for herself. "I feel that I should always be studying and making A's. No matter how much I study, it is never enough," she said. "It seems I can never let myself relax. I should always be doing something," she added, "otherwise I feel guilty. If I am not studying and if I get a B once in awhile, I get very angry at myself." Anne continued, "At the same time, I want to do other things well. I work 20 hours a week. I also feel I should exercise daily, keep up with my housework, and always look nice." Other women cite similar self-expectations. As they talk, they begin to understand the relationship between setting unrealistic goals and the resulting depression and loss in self-esteem when these goals are not met.

We discuss the self-defeating nature of perfectionism in relation to the binge-purge cycle. Frequently, bulimics set impossible goals for themselves in what they "should" weigh (regardless of what is considered normal for their frames), in how much food they "should" eat, and in how fast they "should" lose weight. Anne again is a typical example. She set her weight goal as 105 lb (unrealistic for her height and bone structure) and fasted in order to reach this goal. This was clearly an impossible task because sooner or later her body needed to be fed, and this led to a binge. She then berated herself for not living up to her goal. In addition, Anne, like other bulimic women, typically set unrealistic goals for the rate at which she should lose weight. Even though she was aware that 1 to 2 lb a week is an adequate weight loss when dieting, she tried to lose 10 lb in two days and became upset when this did not happen. Again, this led to her feeling depressed, guilty, and angry at herself—and eating a bag of cookies to punish herself! It is important to make bulimic women aware of the self-defeating nature of setting such high goals and to emphasize that setting lower and more realistic weight goals results in more weight loss. Again, we reinforce the notion that eating regular meals daily instead of starving leads to more successful weight control.

Although some women may become aware of the self-defeating nature of their thinking and behavior, they may still feel that there are advantages to their perfectionism. We ask them what are the advantages and disadvantages of perfectionism and cite from Burns' (1980) article some of the reported findings, which suggest that perfectionists do not display better performance because they set high goals. In addition to feeling depressed and performing poorly, perfectionists may also be prone to poor health, particularly coronary disease. They are lonely because they are afraid of criticism from others and fear that they will not be accepted if they are less than perfect.

When we talk about perfectionism, we reinforce the previous week's discussion of how our thinking affects our behavior and describe how all-or-nothing thinking and overgeneralization, characteristic of perfectionists, lead to binge eating. Frequently, bulimics are either "on" or "off" a diet. When a bulimic woman is "on" a diet, she starves; when she's "off," she binges. When she eats a cookie after starving herself all day, she may say, "Well, I blew it. I'm off my diet now. I might as well eat the whole bag." Many bulimic women see eating in extremes—dieting or binge eating—with no happy medium. The all-or-nothing thinking is also illustrated in their labeling their day or themselves as "good" or "bad" in relation to their eating habits. A "good" day or "being good" usually means not eating anything all day. If she is "bad," meaning she started the day off with a doughnut, then she may as well continue to be "bad" and binge. This all-or-nothing thinking not only frequently leads to binges but also to feeling depressed and guilty afterwards.

Similar to all-or-nothing thinking is the overgeneralization from one situation to many. For example, Jackie told herself, "If I gain 1 lb, I will gain 5 or 10. I blew it today. I'll always blow it. I ate one piece of cake. I can never control myself." We caution women to become aware of words like "always" and "never" and "ever" in their thinking and to change what they are telling themselves. For example, Jackie could ask herself "Why should I gain 10 lb if I gain 1?" or tell herself "Just because I binged this week doesn't mean I'll never control my binges."

Another type of statement that perfectionists make is the "should" statement. When perfectionists make mistakes, rather than trying to learn from them, many punish themselves by saying, "I shouldn't have done that. I should have known better." These "shoulds" are generally quite harsh and lead to guilt and feelings of inadequacy. We conduct a group exercise in which we ask women to list their "shoulds" and then we write them on the board (Figure 5.1). Women tend to place high demands on themselves (e.g. "I should be skinny, I should be able to do everything and do it well," and so on). We ask women to challenge their "shoulds." For example: What is studying more? How many hours of studying per week is enough? How can they do everything and do it well? We encourage them to lower their expectations so that they can meet their goals more readily and have a feeling of accomplishment. We tell them to make their "should" statements more realistic. For example, rather than saying, "I should be more organized," they can state "I would like to clean my desk within the next week." We may point out to them that by being more

FIGURE 5.1. "I Should"

1.

2.

3.

4.

5.

6.

7.

8.

9.

10.

specific in stating a goal, it is easier to attain. "Cleaning a desk" is clearly definable and concrete, whereas "becoming more organized" is abstract and difficult to identify.

Many women may resist lowering their expectations because they assume that only by setting the highest possible goals will they perform well. However, they need to realize that frequently the goals they are setting are impossible to attain and that this only leads to discouragement. If they aim for more modest achievements, the chances are that they will accomplish their goals and may even exceed them.

NOURISHING OURSELVES WITHOUT FOOD

We encourage women to replace their "should" statements by "wants" and discuss how they can "nourish" themselves in ways that do not require food. In another exercise, we ask them to write down which situations make them feel good, which relationships are nourishing, and what they can say and do to make themselves feel good (Figure 5.2). Many bulimics, as we noted before, are extremely harsh on themselves and do not treat themselves with the kindness that they would treat others. Connie, who was typical of many of our group members, was so busy "feeding" everyone else, she was not taking care of herself. Although some women may feel that taking care of their needs is "selfish," we point out that being "selfish" means loving and taking care of yourself. If we are good to ourselves and nourish ourselves with rest and gentleness, then we have the energy and resources to give to others as well. We ask women to think of other ways they can "nourish" themselves or give themselves a "treat" besides food. Buying clothes or perfume for themselves, taking a bubble bath, listening to music, reading the entire newspaper, and taking a nap were some of the "treats" mentioned by women. Talking to themselves nicely, such as "you did a good job" and "you're doing the best you can," is another form of nourishment. We encourage women to "feed" themselves positive thoughts instead of critical ones. Friends also serve as "nourishers," and women are encouraged to cultivate those relationships that make them feel good about themselves.

RAISING SELF-ESTEEM

Another exercise is designed to raise self-esteem and to counteract some of the harshness with which bulimics frequently judge themselves. This exercise is adapted from Morris and Shelton's (1974) "Ego Tripping." Each woman lists five qualities that she likes about herself (Figure 5.3).

FIGURE 5.2. How Can I Nourish Myself?

1. What situations make me feel good? (Make sure you put "fun" things here, not goal directed activities such as "being prepared for class," etc.)

2. Which relationships are nourishing? Why?

3. What do I *say* and *do* to make myself feel good? Make a list and keep adding to it.

FIGURE 5.3. My Positive Qualities

1.

2.

3.

4.

5.

What Others Like About Me
Colleague:

Family Member:

Friend:

After she lists her positive qualities, group members provide her with further feedback about what they like about her. This helps raise self-esteem as well as encourages interaction among group members. In individual therapy, the therapist can provide the woman with some feedback and add to her list of positive qualities.

The homework for this session is basically a continuation of the work they have done in the session. We ask each woman to read the David Burns' article on perfectionism and to add to her "I Should," nourishing activities, and positive qualities lists. She is also to choose one nourishing activity from her list to do this week. To remind women to "nourish" themselves daily we ask each one to get an attractive box. We ask her to write down each nourishing activity on a small piece of paper, fold the paper, and put it in the box. She is to go to the box and take out a piece of paper each time she is tempted to nourish herself by binge eating. She is then to do that activity instead of binge eating. This is an effective exercise and has an element of fun and surprise in it. In addition, she is to ask three people (one who knows her at work or at school, one family member, and one friend) to tell her what they like about her and then she must record that.

This homework assignment has been successful in helping women feel better about themselves. Although many women are reluctant at first to ask their family and friends what they like about them, most are glad they did. We recognize the fear and embarrassment at asking others for positive feedback and attempt to minimize those feelings by suggesting to the woman that she tell others she is doing this as part of a homework assignment.

Some women, like Donna, come back with tears in their eyes as they report the positive statements others have made about them. "I must be worth something, I never realized that I had so many good qualities," she said. "It really felt so good to hear the same thing from so many people," said many of the other women. We encourage them to look at this list over and over, especially when they are feeling bad about themselves. They may even wish to frame it! Some women will not do this assignment the first time. We ask them to do it for the next week. This has proven to be quite effective in boosting self-esteem, and we strongly encourage women to ask the people in their lives to tell them what they like about them.

SUMMARY

1. Go over homework for Week 2.
2. Discuss the relationship between depression, self-esteem, and perfectionism and how they apply to the binge-purge cycle.

3. Have women list their "shoulds" and discuss how these affect their behavior.
4. Help women find ways of "nourishing" themselves without food, through discussion of situations, people, and thoughts and actions that raise self-esteem.
5. Have each woman list at least five positive qualities about herself. In groups, she can receive feedback from others as to what they like about her.
6. Give the homework for Week 3.

HOMEWORK

1. Read "The Perfectionist's Script for Self-Defeat" by David Burns, appearing in *Psychology Today*, November 1980.
2. Add to your lists of "I Shoulds," "How Can I Nourish Myself," and "My Positive Qualities," (Figures 5.1, 5.2, 5.3).
3. Choose one thing from your list of nourishing activities and do it. If you would like to be reminded of "nourishing" activities daily, here is an exercise you might like to try. Get an attractive box and write down each nourishing activity you can think of on a small piece of paper, fold the paper, and put it in the box. Go to your box and take out a piece of paper each time you are tempted to binge. Do whatever is on that paper. Then fold it up again and put it in the box. Keep adding to your box of "treats."
4. Ask three people (one who knows you at work or at school, one family member, and one friend) to tell you what they like about you and record it. This maybe difficult to do but do it anyway. You may tell them that you are doing this for a class if it will make it easier for you.
5. Continue your binge diary (see Appendix).

Chapter 6
Week 4—Anger and Assertiveness

RELATIONSHIP OF ANGER AND ASSERTIVENESS TO BULIMIA

In chapter 1, we reviewed some of the research findings that indicate binge eating is often precipitated by a difficulty in handling negative emotional states, such as anger or anxiety (Abraham & Beumont, 1982; Katzman & Wolchik, 1983a; Leon et al., 1985; Pyle et al., 1981). Our clinical observations of bulimic women were consistent with those findings. Many of the bulimic women we saw appeared to have difficulty expressing their emotions directly or assertively. Frequently, they ate instead of focusing on what was "eating" them.

Although our measurement of assertiveness did not reflect differences between bulimics, binge eaters, and normals (Katzman & Wolchik, 1984), other authors (Boskind-White & White, 1983) have hypothesized that assertion deficits are a central component of bulimia and are related to stereotypic "feminine" behavior, such as dependency and passivity. The exact relationship of bulimia to assertion is not clear, but helping women to express their feelings directly rather than eating as a result of them is one of the goals of our program. Assertiveness skills can help the bulimic woman overcome her limited coping skills, as well as her depression and low self-esteem.

Anger appears to be one of the emotions that is difficult to express assertively and directly. Our language has many expressions relating anger to eating behavior. We frequently hear people talking about "swallowing" their feelings or feeling "fed up." "I can't digest this," "he makes me puke," "I ended up eating my words," "swallowing my pride" and other expressions frequently creep into peoples' vocabularies when they discuss

65

their anger. Anne discussed the direct relationship between her anger and her binge eating and purging: "I swallow my anger and then I spit it up," she said. "Stuffing" can refer to the bulimic episode as well as to the containment of feelings.

In this session, we discuss the relationship of anger and assertiveness to binge eating. In their binge diaries for the previous sessions women have provided numerous examples of when they have binged instead of dealing with their feelings assertively. For example, Donna recounted that she binged whenever she talked to her mother on the phone. Her mother would frequently make comments that angered her; however, rather than express her feelings, she would hang up the phone and go to the refrigerator instead. Other women reported being unable to stand up to boyfriends, husbands, or bosses and ended up dealing with their feelings by "stuffing" themselves. Frequently, women overeat when they feel overworked and drained because they are unable to say "no" to the demands of others.

ASSERTIVENESS

What is Assertiveness?

We provide a brief introduction to assertiveness in this session and review the differences between assertive, nonassertive, and aggressive behavior (Alberti & Emmons, 1970). We encourage women to express their feelings assertively, that is, in an open and direct manner without hurting themselves or hurting anyone else. We tell them that assertiveness is frequently confused with aggressive behavior, which is also open expression of feelings but expression usually done at the expense of someone else. When a person doesn't express her feelings and lets others step all over her, she is behaving nonassertively. We discuss the fact that at different times and with different people each woman may behave either assertively, aggressively, or nonassertively. Some women provide examples of when they alternate between acting "bitchy" and "like a mouse" in their relationships. Others recount that they can tell some friends anything they want but become tongue-tied around others.

Human Rights

Because behaving assertively frequently involves exercising our rights, we ask women to make a list of their basic human rights. Many women do not express themselves because they may not be aware that they have these rights. After listing these on the board, we discuss how they might exercise their rights more. We read over the list of Assertive Human Rights in Manuel Smith's book *When I Say No, I Feel Guilty* (1975). These include the right to judge our own behavior, to make mistakes, to change our mind, and to say "I don't know," "I don't care," or "I don't understand." Other human rights are the right to express ourselves as long as we don't hurt others, to refuse a request without feeling guilty, to express anger, and to have our opinions respected.

Saying No

One of the rights that many women do not exercise is that of saying "no" without feeling guilty about it. We discussed in the previous chapter how many bulimics feel they are being "selfish" if they do not put other peoples' needs ahead of their own. For example, Connie felt she could not say "no" to anyone who asked for help. She was involved in too many activities and was finding it increasingly difficult to keep up with her schoolwork and daily chores. She was feeling fatigued, run-down, and depressed. The group asked her which of the many activities she had taken on could she give up. However, she felt that she would be unable to let go of any of them. She wanted to be able to do everything. After some time, she was able to accept her limitations and give up some of her extracurricular activities.

Living up to an image is one of the reasons why many women say "yes" when they would really like to say "no" to requests. As in the above example, many women want to believe that they should be able to do everything. We urge women to explore their reasons for saying "yes" instead of "no" to requests. Jackie's reasons are similar to other women's: "I'm afraid that people will think that I'm not capable if I say I can't do something. I want people to say, 'Look at her. She can handle anything.'" Other women frequently report that they want to prove to themselves or to others that they can do everything. As we did in the previous session on perfectionism, we encourage women to lower their expectations and not to attempt to be perfect. This can be most effective when done with humor. For example, after a woman berates herself for being unable to keep up with all the demands she makes on herself, the therapist can sigh an exaggerated sigh of relief and wipe her brow, as she states "Whew! For a while there I was really getting worried. I thought Superwoman came back to earth! I'm so glad you are human after all!"

When women say "yes" only to end up feeling exploited and angry, they are probably saying "yes" for the wrong reasons. One of the most common reasons is to win acceptance and approval. Women report that they are afraid that if they refuse someone's request, the other person will stop liking them. We try to reassure them that some people are not going to like them regardless of what they do, and in fact, sometimes too much niceness can make others uncomfortable. We tell them that we don't need everyone's approval, but if we assert ourselves, we may get their respect, and that is more important. We encourage women to experiment by being more assertive, and they are usually surprised to find that they seldom get any of their anticipated negative consequences from others.

Some women report that they say "yes" instead of "no" to avoid hurting someone's feelings. However, by doing something that they do not really want to, their unwillingness may become apparent and result in the hurt feelings that they were trying to avoid in the first place. For example, Celia frequently went out with friends she didn't like just so she could be "polite." However, she resented being with them so much that she generally acted quiet, and her sulking was interpreted as rudeness.

Another wrong reason for saying "yes" for some women is to convince themselves that they are "okay," or normal, that there is nothing wrong. They try to make up for real or imagined failures and end up feeling exploited. Claire, for example, always gave in to her five-year-old son and gave him practically everything he asked for. She was afraid to say "no" to his requests for her time, attention, toys, or whatever else he asked for. Like many working mothers, she felt guilty for leaving him alone and then tried to make it up to him by overindulging him.

We let women explore their own reasons for saying "yes" when they wish to say "no" and then use role play to help them with difficult situations. The role play is generally effective, and many receive feedback from other group members. Sometimes the therapist can model effective assertive behavior. When we use role play, we make use of several guidelines. We tell each woman that she has a right to say "no" without feeling guilty, and that, with practice, this can become a habit. We also remind her that saying "no" does not mean rejecting the other person, but is simply refusing a request. We encourage assertive, positive, and appropriate body language. We tell them that when saying "no" it is important to be direct and to the point and not to be swayed by guilt, pleading, threats, or other forms of manipulation. The other person is generally aware of a weak "no" and will use any method to change that to a "yes." In some cases, the woman may have to use the broken record technique, which is simply saying "no" over and over calmly without being distracted by side issues. The role play can be fun for group members and build group cohesiveness. Interjecting humor into the role play makes it less threatening.

Expressing Anger

A specific assertiveness skill that is difficult for many women is that of expressing anger directly rather than "stuffing it in" or "spitting it out." We ask women to think of a specific situation in which they felt angry and did not express their anger the way they wanted to. They could have either overreacted or underreacted in the situation, but in either case, they were unhappy with how they handled it. We ask them to write down their responses to the following questions about that specific situation: (a) To whom was my anger directed? (b) What did I actually do or say? (c) What did I want to do or say? (d) What were my fears behind saying or doing what I wanted to?

In providing responses to these questions, women become aware of how they handle their anger and their fears behind expressing themselves in the manner that they wanted.

"I asked my brother when he was going to give me back the money I lent him. He started calling me so many dirty names. I was stunned. I was afraid I was going to hit him or that I would start to cry; so I just walked out of the room shaking," said Delores, one of the women in our program.

"My date was over an hour late. I was really mad and would have liked to say something to him, but I pretended it was okay. I was afraid if I told him how I really felt, he'd get angry at me and never ask me out again," said Jackie.

"My best friend asked me to babysit for her kids for the umpteenth time. I was angry at her for taking me for granted and wanted to tell her to get her own babysitter but I felt I was being petty, and I didn't think it was nice to feel that way, so I kept quiet," added Celia.

In these and other examples, women recounted that fears of their reaction or of other peoples' reactions to anger prevented them from speaking up. They were afraid that they would either lose control by crying, yelling, or saying something they would regret later. They were also afraid of reprisal if they became angry, afraid that the other person would either stop caring for them or would retaliate in anger as well. In addition, many women have been brought up to believe that it is not "nice" to feel angry and resentful, and they have learned to repress their feelings. For some women, anger is so threatening that they can not recall a single instance in which they felt angry.

The therapist needs to assure these women that anger is a normal and healthy emotion, and that anger and violence are not synonymous, as many people believe. Anger can be expressed quietly and tactfully, without being rude or losing control. Further, the therapist can reassure the women that expressing anger is a choice; that, in certain situations, one may choose not to state her feelings. For example, negative consequences may result if a woman expresses her anger to some authority figures who may become overly defensive and retaliate if provoked even slightly. However, in most situations, anger, if assertively expressed, can be constructive.

Role play can also be done in this session to help women rehearse difficult situations. Some guidelines for helping women to express their anger assertively are to have their words, voice, and facial expression match. Many women will smile while they are saying that they are angry, thus undermining the effectiveness of their message. Expressing anger with "I" rather than with "you" statements also tends to make the communication more effective and less threatening to the other person. For example, she can state "I feel angry right now" instead of "you make me so mad." The "you" messages suggest blame and may be construed as aggressive rather than assertive communications.

Although we encourage the expression of anger, in some situations women may choose to control their inner rage so that they can speak politely and assertively instead of striking out. We teach women to use messages to calm themselves down so that they can express themselves confidently. We have already discussed with them in previous sessions how talking to themselves and changing the way they think can influence their behavior, and we apply this to anger situations as well. We provide examples of how changing their thinking about a situation can calm them down so that they can behave more assertively. For example, if someone is provoking a woman and she tells herself, "That creep! He's really getting to me!" she is likely to become more enraged. If instead she tells herself, "I'll just let him make a fool of himself," she is not as likely to become upset. We give them some examples of self-statements in stress inoculation training for controlling anger (Novaco, 1975) and ask them which of these statements they can use. Novaco cites examples of statements to make when preparing for provocation (e.g., "This is going to upset me, but I know how to deal with it," "Try not to take this too seriously"); at the time of confrontation (e.g., "Stay calm, just continue to relax," "I'm not going to let him get to me"); when coping with arousal (e.g., "Time to take a deep breath," "I'll let him make a fool of himself"); as well as when reflecting on the provocation when the conflict is unresolved (e.g., "Don't take it personally") or resolved (e.g., "I handled that one pretty well. It worked!").

For homework, we continue the work on anger by asking them to keep a record of situations in which they felt angry and how they handled these. This is designed to help them get further in touch with their angry feelings. For women who are participating in the group program, it may be appropriate to schedule the second individual session, particularly if they are having difficulty expressing anger to others. For homework, they are to review the material on assertiveness discussed in the group and they are given an assignment called "Yes's and No's" adapted from Lonnie Barbach (1975).

According to Barbach (1980), the Yes-and-No exercise is the single most useful exercise she has found with psychotherapy clients with low self-esteem. The exercise involves asking the woman to say "no" to three things she did not want to do but would ordinarily agree to do, and to say "yes" to three things she would like to do but ordinarily would not accept. In both cases, the woman is being given permission to do what she really wanted to do anyway. The "yes's" are essentially an extension of the "nourishing activities," those ways of enhancing herself and telling herself that she is a worthwhile person, one who deserves to do nice things for herself. The "no's" are getting rid of the unrealistic "shoulds" and treating herself more kindly. This exercise affects the woman's self-esteem and sense of power and reverses her pattern of neglecting herself. Many bulimic women would not ordinarily "treat" themselves to something nice. However, being trained to be "good" girls, they follow the therapists' suggestions, which gives them permission to try new behaviors. Furthermore, they see that the consequences of assertive behavior are not as harsh as they anticipated.

SUMMARY

1. Review the homework from the previous week and focus on examples where women binged instead of expressed their feelings assertively. Ask them what was "eating" them when they ate. Briefly discuss the relationship between binge eating and assertiveness and anger.
2. Review basic assertiveness concepts and differentiate between assertive, nonassertive, and aggressive behavior.
3. Ask women to list their human rights and encourage them to exercise those rights.
4. Discuss the right to say "no" without feeling guilty and help women explore their reasons for saying "yes" when they wish to say "no." Role-play if appropriate.
5. Ask women to list situations in which they did not handle anger appropriately. Discuss guidelines for expressing anger and role-play if needed.
6. Give homework for Week 4, and schedule an individual session for those women who may need extra work at this point.

HOMEWORK

1. Review the material on assertiveness, basic human rights, saying "no," and expressing anger. Review the definitions on assertiveness in Alberti and Emmon's book *Your Perfect Right* (1970), the basic human rights and guidelines on saying "no" listed in Smith's book *When I Say No, I Feel Guilty* (1975), and the self-statements in stress inoculation training for controlling anger (Novaco, 1975, pp. 166–167).
2. This exercise is adapted from Lonnie Barbach (1975) and is called the "Yes's and No's." Say "no" to three things that you didn't want to

do but felt that you should do. This could be to someone else or to yourself. For example, you can say "no" to babysitting for your niece when you don't feel like it, or you can say "no" to going out with someone you don't like when you don't want to. You can also say "no" to doing the laundry or cleaning up your closet when you feel like doing something else. Say "yes" to three things that you really want but would usually not let yourself have or ask others for. You can buy that new dress or new book that you wanted but didn't feel you could let yourself have, or you can go ahead and sleep an extra hour or take that luxurious bath you don't have time for. Or you can let your friends do something nice for you. Record these below.

No's

1.

2.

3.

Yes's

1.

2.

3.

3. Note situations this week in which you felt angry and how you handled them. Record these. How did you feel you handled them? What changes do you need to make?

Situations that Made Me Angry	How I Handled Them

4. Continue your binge diary (see Appendix).

Chapter 7

Week 5—Cultural
Expectations of Thinness
for Women

SOCIETAL EXPECTATIONS
FOR THINNESS

This week's session focuses on how societal expectations for women to be "slim" and "feminine" lead them to binge eat and purge. The remark, "You can never be too rich or too thin," reportedly made by the Duchess of Windsor, encapsulates what society's expectations of thinness for women are. Orbach (1978) eloquently discusses cultural demands on women to be slim and to fit certain standards. She states that our culture emphasizes physical appearance as a central aspect of a woman's existence. As a result, the woman becomes self-conscious when she compares herself to the image of the "ideal woman" presented by the media. In trying to live up to this image, she becomes a victim of the diet and fashion industry that tries to remold her body to fit the "ideal" body type. According to messages from the media, the woman's body is unacceptable the way it is and must be constantly remodeled, deodorized, perfumed, and freed of excess hair. This job of refashioning women's bodies is constant, for the "ideal" body type changes from year to year. Just as styles in clothes change every season, so are women's bodies expected to change. One year, the voluptuous, bosomy woman is "in;" the next, the thin, "Twiggy" type model is in fashion. One factor remains constant in these changing images: that a woman remain slim.

In this session, we elicit a discussion of these cultural demands for slimness and help women become aware of their feelings about these demands. Anne appeared to be speaking for most of the women when she described how it seemed to her that she could never open a magazine, turn on the television, or see an ad without this image of the ideal, model-slim woman being presented. Like other women, she expressed her anger at her inability to make her body conform to these standards despite her stringent dieting and purging. For Anne and for others, the binge-purge behavior is frequently related to their wish to look like the model-slim ideal type.

THE "PERFECT WOMAN"

We do three exercises in this session to help women become aware of the unrealistic societal expectations for thinness and how it affects their behavior. Because being thin is one constant in the image of the ideal woman, we ask women to list the qualities of the "Perfect Woman" as depicted by our society. We tell them to take a few minutes to visualize the perfect woman. What does she look like? What is she like? We write down their responses on the board as they say them. Some of the characteristics usually attributed to the perfect woman are physical. First and foremost, she must be tall and thin. With today's emphasis on physical fitness and exercise, a firm and muscular body is also important in the definition of the perfect woman. Long legs, a flat abdomen, and looking healthy are also mentioned. In addition, she must have a tan; white even teeth; as well as "flawless" skin without wrinkles, pimples, or blemishes. Other features include youth—the perfect woman is usually in her early twenties. Smooth legs and arms without any hair are also associated with the ideal woman. In addition, "perfect" features are important in the definition (i.e., a straight nose, large eyes, long lashes, and a round mouth). She must always be immaculately groomed, not a hair out of place, her make-up perfect, and her clothes must be the latest styles. She looks wonderful at all times and she does all this effortlessly. Variations of these statements are made by women. In addition to physical attributes, a perfect woman is bright, has a successful career, and a successful personal life. She is an intelligent woman, who is also a gourmet cook, and a wonderful wife and mother. To sum up, the perfect woman should do "everything well" and do it "effortlessly."

Such an unrealistic image of woman only exists on television. This exercise generally brings laughter from women as they become aware of the absurdity of trying to live up to an unrealistic image of Superwoman, and feeling depressed and disappointed when they do not. The therapist can inject some humor into this exercise to make it more effective and meaningful.

PAYOFFS AND PRICE OF
STRIVING TO BE PERFECT

A second exercise is designed to make them aware of the payoffs and price of trying to live up to this ideal image. We ask women to list the advantages and disadvantages of trying to live up to this Superwoman image, and we write their responses on the board. Attention from men, feelings of confidence, and admiration from others are frequently listed as the benefits of trying to live up to this ideal. Women report, "I feel I can lick the world if I am feeling gorgeous," "When I really feel I look my best, then I get lots of male attention," "I like others to think I'm Superwoman, even if I'm not. I like to be admired by others for being so slim and doing everything well."

We tell women that attention and admiration from others and feeling confident and good about themselves are certainly good payoffs. However, we ask if the payoffs make the excessive dieting worthwhile. What, we ask, are the disadvantages of trying to live up to this image? How do they abuse themselves and their bodies to be Superwomen? We ask women to list the price they pay in their efforts to reach this goal, and we put their responses on the board. Women list their health, their ability to have fun, their emotions, their identity, and their friendships as being affected by their attempt to be the perfect woman.

Responses such as these are typical:

"When I think of what I have done to my body, just so I can fit into a certain size, I shudder. I get scared when I think of all the physical problems I can have and what this can do to my health," said Anne.

"I feel starved and deprived most of the time. I'm also tired and irritable. I don't like feeling this way," Donna added.

"I feel insecure all the time. I worry that people only like me for my looks," said Penny.

"I get depressed because no matter what I do, I will never be thin enough and never look like the perfect woman," Delores reported.

"I don't have fun any more because I'm always worrying about how I look," Jackie added.

"I don't go out with friends because then I might eat and gain weight," said Celia.

This exercise can serve as an eye-opener, as the price of trying to look perfect is very high. We stress to women that looking good *is* important. It is the *excessive* time and effort that they spend on this aspect of their life that is self-defeating. The time and effort in thinking, planning, and worrying about that extra pound could be spent in more important ways.

BEHAVIOR AROUND MEN

We do a third exercise to help women become aware of how societal expectations to be the perfect woman also extend to how they relate to men. As we have discussed previously, the role of sex-role difficulties and heterosexual difficulties has been suggested as central to bulimia (Boskind-White & White, 1983). We ask women to write down how they behave when they are around other women and how they behave when they are around men whom they find attractive. Although many women intellectually rejected the stereotype of "feminine" behavior (e.g., demure, deferential, passive) and felt that it didn't apply to them, they were surprised to find that they related differently to men than they did to women. Penny, for example, prided herself on being a "liberated" woman. However, she was startled to discover that she frequently did not express her desires and preferences around men as much as she did around women. When a man asked her what movie she wanted to see or where she wanted to go out for dinner, she told him what she thought he wanted to hear. This is, in fact, similar to Rost et al.'s (1982) findings that although bulimics may have "liberated" attitudes, their actual behavior represents an adaption of their behavior to the traditional role concept of passivity, dependency, and underassertiveness. They hypothesize that this discrepancy is a source of stress and may even precipitate a binge. Given the women's perfectionism, it is likely that failure to live up to sex-role ideals occurs and results in some depression.

Women reported feeling more self-conscious around men than women, as expressed by these statements:

"I'm more conscious of the way I look and act when I'm around men, particularly those I find attractive. I'm not as comfortable with men," said Clara.

"If I'm with a man I find very attractive, I blush or stutter. With women, I can be myself more," Donna added.

"I'm always aware that he's watching me and so I'm more stilted and awkward," Penny stated.

"I'm more coy around men, doing what I think they will like, doing things to get their approval," said Jackie.

Women reported performing for men and trying to please men. They were usually more open with women. The times they didn't trust other women were generally when they were competing for a man's approval. Through this exercise, women may gain some insight into how much of their behavior reflects their view of men as evaluators and of themselves as products to be evaluated. In their efforts to be products that would be evaluated positively by men, they subject their bodies to the stringent dieting and purging.

We have women identify some of the ways they behave differently around men than they behave around women and see if they want to change any of those behaviors. We ask them to study which of these behaviors are advantageous for them to keep and which are not. We do not ask them to change long-term patterns of behavior, just to become aware of them. After becoming aware of their behavior around men, they can then choose which behaviors they want to keep and which they wish to change. They may wish to practice new behaviors and see if these are more effective in how they relate to men and in how they feel about themselves. They may want to experiment in small steps, for example, consciously not attempting to be "witty" or "perform" for a man. Is there a difference in the way they feel? In the way he relates to them? Or they may wish to express their preferences the next time a man asks them which movie they want to see instead of saying what they think will please him.

Through the discussions and exercises in this session, we hope that women will become aware of the self-defeating nature of trying to conform to an impossible image. We encourage them to stop trying to live up to an unrealistic ideal and to learn to accept themselves and their bodies as they are. Rather than trying to become the perfect woman, they can start accepting and loving their bodies, with "unwanted" hair, pimples, wrinkles, and all, even if they don't conform to what's "in" this year.

The homework for this week is geared to enhancing body image and leads into the next week's discussion. The first homework exercise is adapted from Lonnie Barbach's (1975) Body Mirror Exercise in which women are asked to examine their bodies without any clothing in front of a full length mirror and list what they like about them. There is usually some resistance to this exercise related to the anticipated discomfort they will feel when doing this. In one group, this discomfort was manifested by several minutes of hysterical laughter as women anticipated looking at themselves. The therapist needs to be aware of how much emotional discomfort underlies this exercise and how much pain women experience because their bodies are not perfect. We tell them we realize this will be difficult for them to do, but it is essential that they do it. Using humor here can be helpful, and the therapist can demonstrate, exaggerating on any negative body parts. The therapist can ask each woman what part of her body will be most difficult to look at and ask her to exaggerate that part in front of the mirror (e.g., stick out her tummy, wiggle her hips, etc.). This exercise may need to be repeated several times until a woman becomes more comfortable with her body. As Jackie put it after several times of doing this exercise, "Now I can get to looking up to my knees. That's progress because I couldn't accept anything before. Next time I'll try to accept the part up to my thighs."

The second homework exercise is to help them become aware that factors other than weight define a person's attractiveness to the opposite sex. They are to ask three men which women they consider sexy or attractive (movie stars and models excluded) and why.

The third homework exercise is designed to help them become aware of some distortions in their body image. They are asked to find a magazine photo of someone whose body they think looks like theirs and one of someone whose body they wish to look like. They are to bring these to the group for feedback. If the client is being seen in individual therapy, she can ask her friends for feedback. Continuation of the binge diary is also given for homework.

SUMMARY

1. Review the homework for Week 4 and go over women's "yes's" and "no's."
2. Briefly discuss how societal expectations of thinness for women lead to binge eating and purging.
3. Ask women to list the qualities of the perfect woman and write those on the board.
4. Ask them to list the payoffs and price of trying to live up to this ideal and write those on the board. Discuss the implications for them.
5. To help women become aware of how societal expectations to be the perfect woman extend to their relationships with men, ask them to write down how they act around other women and how they act around men. Discuss the implications for them.
6. Encourage women to stop trying to live up to an impossible ideal and to learn to accept themselves and their bodies as they are.
7. Give them the homework for this session.

HOMEWORK

1. Read pages 20–21 from Susie Orbach's book *Fat is a Feminist Issue* (1978), which discusses societal expectations for slimness for women.
2. Do the Body Mirror Exercise (Barbach, 1975). Take an hour when you can be uninterrupted and insured of privacy. Set up a full length mirror in the privacy of your room or bathroom. Get into a relaxed mood by taking a bubble bath, listening to music, and/or drinking a glass of wine. Stand in front of the mirror and look at your body from all sides and angles. Talk to yourself as you look, telling yourself what you like, starting from your hair and going down to your toes. If there are some parts you don't care for, such as a protruding stomach or "love handles," exaggerate those by sticking them out until you are comfortable

with them. You may have to do this exercise several times over the next weeks until you feel comfortable with your body. Record on the provided sheet what you like about your body. Keep adding to your list.

What I Like About My Body

3. Ask three men to tell you which women they consider sexy and why. Ask them to pick women you know or point to someone (movie stars and models excluded). Record your reactions to what they say. Are you surprised by what you hear? Why? This exercise is designed to help you become aware of what others consider sexy or attractive. Many women are surprised to discover that fairly average looking women who do not fit the perfect woman image are considered sexy or attractive by men. They are also surprised to find out that factors other than weight are mentioned in defining a person's attractiveness.

Who Is Sexy and Attractive   *Why*   *My Reactions*

1.

2.

3.

4. Find a magazine photo of someone whose body you think looks like yours and one of someone whose body you wish to look like and bring these to the next session. Ask your friends for feedback. Most women see themselves as much chunkier than others see them. Many women have a distorted picture of their body and view it more negatively than do others. Ask your friends for a more realistic picture of yourself. Learn to see yourself more realistically.
5. Continue your binge diary (see Appendix).

Chapter 8
Week 6—Enhancing Body Image

BULIMIA AND BODY IMAGE

How women feel about their bodies is an emotional issue, and for many women, regardless of their size and shape, their bodies tend to be a source of anxiety and hurt. Bulimic women in particular experience a great deal of emotional pain in their perceptions of their bodies. As noted at the beginning of this book, bulimic women report being preoccupied with their weight and body size (Fairburn, 1980; Palmer, 1979; Russell, 1979; Wermuth et al., 1977). In addition, our research findings suggest that they have a poorer body image in comparison to normals and binge eaters (Katzman & Wolchik, 1984). In our work with these women, we have found them to have very negative feelings about their bodies.

We discussed in the last chapter how the media and designers of women's clothing set different standards of what a woman should look like each year. Some years the curvaceous look is promoted, in contrast to other years, where the tall, willowy look is displayed on all magazine covers. If a woman is not this year's model, she feels like a failure. A body can be in fashion one year and out of fashion the next. Trying to rearrange and remold the body to fit the times is absurd. However, many women go to considerable lengths to do just that and experience a great deal of anguish in trying to go against the natural contours of their bodies.

Even when there is agreement as to what constitutes a beautiful body, the truth for most women is that they will not look like the models depicted on magazine covers regardless of how much weight they lose or whatever other "improvements" they make in their physical appearance. They could spare themselves much anxiety and pain if they could accept their bodies as they are instead of reaching for unrealistic and impossible standards.

In trying to attain these impossible goals, women frequently deny some of the realities of body shape and function and try to go against their natural body contours. Anne expressed it this way: ''All the women in my family have large rounded breasts and thighs. We are not really fat, just curvy. Yet I keep trying to look like a beanpole! I know that no matter what I do, I won't look like a skinny model simply because this is my body shape—I wonder why I'm trying to change nature.''

Anne, similar to many other women, kept trying to get rid of her ''rounded'' stomach (she had a flat stomach by almost anyone's standards). She wanted her stomach to look ''concave,'' even though she said ''I know that is not anatomically possible, but I still want my tummy to be sucked in.'' Despite her awareness that she was trying to fit her body into an artificial mold, she still felt depressed over her ''imperfections.''

Anne's feelings about her body are similar to those of many bulimic women. They feel depressed about and ashamed of their bodies and let that interfere with their deriving pleasure from it. Many women report that their feelings about their bodies interfere with sexual enjoyment because they won't allow their partners to look at them or touch them. This self-consciousness about the body leading to less enjoyment of sex was supported in a study by Alderdissen et al. (1981) comparing bulimic and normal women on a variety of psychological measures. Bulimics reported less enjoyment of sexual relationships, a greater difficulty in expressing their sexual wishes, and more fear of not meeting their partner's sexual expectations. Additionally, they held to a greater degree the belief that their satisfaction of sex would improve if they were slimmer and more attractive. The negative feelings about their bodies and lack of sexual satisfaction may lead some women to binge, substituting food for sex and love. Unfortunately, the binge eating further reinforces the negative feelings about the body. Several women have reported using binge eating as a substitute for sexual satisfaction and intimacy.

GOALS OF THE SESSION

In this session, we review the homework exercises from the previous session to help women see their bodies more positively and realistically. The exercises in this session are more effective when done in a group because feedback and confrontation from others are important. The feedback and confrontation provide insight for these women on their distorted body images and on how others perceive them, which is usually much less critical than the way they perceive themselves. Women gain insight into their own behavior by observing other group members. When the woman is seen individually, anecdotal material and feedback from therapist and friends helps her see her body more realistically and feel better about it.

There are several goals for this session: (a) to enhance body image, (b) to help women realize that weight is not the only physical criterion for attractiveness, (c) to show that *behaviors* and not only *appearance* are important in defining one's attractiveness, and (d) to help women become aware of and decrease distortions in body image. The homework exercises from the previous week and the exercises in the group are done to help them correct their negative perceptions of themselves and to feel better about their bodies.

Enhancing Body Image: Review of the Body Mirror Exercise

Women recount what they liked about their appearance when they looked in the mirror. They are asked to stand in front of the group and validate their bodies, telling the group what they liked about them. They are not to mention anything they did not like. If group members have difficulty doing this at first, the therapist can model as she stands up and goes through each of her own body parts, starting from the top of her head and ending with her toes. It is important that the therapist does not mention weight when doing this exercise, but focuses more on the "functional" qualities of her features (e.g., "I love my hair because it is so easy to manage," "I like my hands because they are so agile," "I like my eyes because they are so expressive," "I like my breasts because they feel so good when they are touched," etc.). What we hope to accomplish here is to have women "own" their bodies, imperfections and all, and feel comfortable with them. When the client does this exercise and tends to skip certain body parts, we encourage her to go back to those parts and validate them. If she qualifies her statements, tending to discount them (e.g., "My hair is nice when I set it" or "My smile is pretty except for my crooked teeth"), we point out that a feature does not have to be perfect to be liked. We encourage her to go back and say, "I like my smile," "I like my pretty hair," etc. When she mentions a nice feature (e.g., "I have nice ankles"), we ask her to talk about it and show us what it looks like from all angles. Essentially, we attempt to reinforce positive responses.

This may seem artificial, and some women may have a very difficult time not saying anything negative about their bodies. We are not asking them to lie about their feelings, only to focus on positive aspects because they have "tunnel vision" and focus only on negatives. If they have a real problem with a certain body part, we ask them to exaggerate that, both in the group and in doing body work at home, until they can feel comfortable with it. For example, they are to stick out their stomach or wiggle their thighs and keep looking at them until some desensitization takes place. They do not necessarily have to like every body part, but they need to feel comfortable with each part. Some aspects of their appearance can be changed, others they have no control over; and they must make friends with their bodies.

After each woman validates her body, group members and therapists give her feedback on what they see as her attractive features. It is important for the therapist not to focus on the woman's thinness except if she has a very distorted body image and sees herself as fat. We also attempt to give feedback on her attractive *behaviors* (e.g., a smile, certain mannerisms, bubbliness, and so on) and not to focus solely on *appearance*. We point out that factors other than physical features, and particularly other than weight, play a role in how others perceive us. Women are surprised to find that when they gave feedback to others, it was the *behaviors* they noticed first rather than the appearance.

The women may not at first accept the feedback; however, as they observe others, they may become aware that they too have been displaying an overly critical attitude towards their own bodies. We tell them to see their bodies through other people's eyes and not through their own critical ones. We encourage them to change their perfectionist attitudes and thoughts about their body parts, and we stress that their bodies do not have to be perfect before they can accept them.

Together with that, we suggest a change in behavior. We urge them to buy clothes for now and not wait until they are perfect (i.e., slim). By giving their bodies the proper attention, they are really saying that they can accept them for now. We ask them to wear "thin clothes" even if they weigh more than they want to. Susie Orbach (1978) challenges the notion that loose clothes make women look smaller than fitted ones. We tell women to dress as they would if they really liked their figures, and gradually they will come to accept their bodies. We ask them to continue doing the Body Mirror Exercise at home until they can learn to accept their bodies and to "own" all of its parts.

Correcting Distortions in Body Image

Being comfortable with one's body also means learning to see it more realistically, without distortions. As we noted at the beginning of the book, bulimics tend to have distortions in body image. For example, bulimic individuals commonly reported an exaggerated fear of becoming obese and a perception of feeling fat when, indeed, they were not (Fairburn & Cooper, 1982; Garfinkel & Garner, 1982; Pyle et al., 1981). The severity of this distortion is highlighted in Fairburn and Cooper's (1982) study in which 63.2% of 499 bulimic women stated their desired weight to be less than 85% of matched population mean weight. Boskind-Lodahl and White (1978) found that all 12 of their subjects in a pilot study manifested a distorted body image.

After women review what they like about their bodies, we ask them to show us the photos they had cut out from magazines of what they *thought* they looked like and what they *wanted* to look like. There is invariably much distortion in how they perceive themselves. Slim or normal weight women bring in pictures of obese women. Group members provide them with feedback about their distortions. Frequently, women are unable to see their own bodies realistically but are incredulous at distortions by other group members. This can provide them with insight into their own perceptions. We tell them that even if they "feel" as though they had "humongous thighs" or "pregnant stomachs," they need to accept intellectually what they look like and take at face value what others tell them.

Through the feedback, group members can correct some of the distortions they have about their bodies. The therapist can give feedback as well, if group members do not. If done with humor, this can be quite effective. For example, as a woman mentions the fat under her arms, the therapist's genuinely incredulous expression and asking "where?" can bring laughter from the group. A woman will obviously not be convinced that she is distorting just because other women tell her she is. However, we ask her to trust other members' perceptions rather than her own, to go by what she *knows* rather than by what she *feels*.

We encourage her to try some reality testing on her own as well, if she is not willing to take other peoples' assessments at face value. She can draw her perceived body outline on a large sheet of paper and then lie down on the paper and ask a friend to trace her actual body outline. The discrepancy between her drawing and her friend's tracing is the extent of distortion. If the feedback indicates that she does indeed have a distorted image of her body, she is to learn to *think* of herself as looking the way she does, even if she still *feels* fat.

Showing that Factors Other than Weight Constitute Attractiveness: What is Sexy?

Not all women distort, of course, and some women *are* overweight, even by the most objective standards. How big a role do their bodies play for others? Is being thin the only way to be attractive? How else can women be attractive or sexy without being thin? The next exercise is designed to bring to their awareness that features other than weight constitute attractiveness to the opposite sex. We ask women to tell us what the men they talked to said they considered sexy or attractive in women, and we write these down on the board. We also ask them to think of what is sexy to them and write that down. Although being thin is mentioned sometimes, personality and behavioral characteristics are noted with even more frequency than physical features. Women are surprised that "average-looking" women with imperfect features are considered sexy. "Sexiness" or "attractiveness" are intangible qualities and do not only include weight or physical appearance. As women tell us what they and others consider sexy we write them on the board. Words used to describe sexiness include, "bright," "in love," "handsome," "athletic," "healthy," "kind," "considerate," "caring," "loving," "self-confident," "talented," "has a sense of humor," "sensitive," "musical," "a good personality," "delivery," "a nice tan," "a good voice," "an 'individual'." Very few of these qualities had to do with weight or even with physical appearance.

As we review the previous week's homework through these exercises, our aims are to help women appreciate their bodies and see them more realistically, as well as to realize that weight, or even physical appearance, is not the sole criterion for attractiveness. We want to stress to bulimic women that there is nothing wrong with self-improvement and wanting to look good. However, it is a problem when self-improvement begins and ends with weight loss. Women have inflated expectations of what being thin will do for them and many postpone living until the day they reach the "perfect" weight. They delay buying clothes, making friends, or doing anything nice for themselves. They feel that everything will fall into place when life begins; in other words, when they lose weight. We try to make them aware of how they have lost perspective, of how dieting has taken over every aspect of their lives. Couldn't the time and effort spent on trying to be thin be put to better use? If they direct their energies to other areas of their lives, *even* to other physical improvements, they may get more satisfaction, and others may see them as more attractive, as well. Those "extra" pounds appear to be a burden on their minds more than on their bodies.

The homework for this session reinforces the work in the group and is again designed to help them like their appearance more and to focus on factors other than weight in feeling good about themselves. They are to write down what they like about their appearance, what others like about it, and what their "attractive behaviors" are. This is to reinforce the feedback they received in the group so that they can refer to it in the future. They are also told to pick one of their "attractive behaviors" from the list and exaggerate it, that is, to change something *behaviorally* that will improve their attractiveness (e.g., to smile more often if it is attractive, to exaggerate certain movements, etc.). They are to record the reactions from others when they deliberately exaggerated these behaviors. They are frequently surprised and delighted to see how much attention they get from males when they are more verbal, smile more, or listen more, when no one notices if they gained or lost a few pounds! They are also asked to change something in their *appearance* aside from losing weight and to record other people's reactions to this change. Again, a change in hairstyle or make-up is likely to bring more comments than the pound or two that is hardly noticed by anyone. In addition, they are to continue their binge diary.

SUMMARY

1. Review the Body Mirror Exercise for each woman. Let her tell the group what she likes about her body and have her receive feedback from other members. In providing feedback, focus on the ''functional'' aspects of the features and on ''behaviors,'' not only on appearance. Help women ''own'' and accept their bodies. Emphasize living and dressing for now.
2. Review the photos and help women correct distortions in body image by getting feedback from others. Encourage group members to go by the feedback rather than by their own perceptions and feelings.
3. Review what is sexy for others and what they find sexy. Bring to awareness that features other than weight define attractiveness and that behaviors and not only appearance make one attractive to the opposite sex.
4. Give homework for this week.

HOMEWORK

This week we will ask you to do three exercises to help you feel better about your body and to become aware of factors other than weight in your attractiveness to others.

1. Write down what you like about your appearance, what others like about it and list your ''attractive behaviors'' below.

What I Like About My Appearance

What Others Like About My Appearance

My ''Attractive Behaviors'' (How else am I attractive aside from appearance?)

2. Pick one of your ''attractive behaviors'' from your list and exaggerate it this week: that is, change something behaviorally that will improve your attractiveness. For example, if people like your smile, make a con-

scious effort to smile more this week. If they like your movements, try exaggerating those. Record the reactions from others to this.

3. Change something in your appearance aside from losing weight. Try a new hairstyle, new make-up, wearing earrings, or anything else aside from weight that will make a difference in your appearance. Record the reactions from others to this.

4. Continue your binge diary.

Chapter 9

Week 7—Summing Up:
Where You Are Now and
Where Do You Go From Here

In the last session of the program, women usually come in with a visible change in appearance, and this is reinforced by therapists and group members. We ask them to relate the reactions from others to the exaggeration of their attractive behaviors and the change in their appearance. We reinforce the notion that factors other than weight constitute attractiveness and get more attention.

The rest of the session is spent reviewing each woman's progress and discussing what she still needs to work on. We frequently give out a questionnaire to help them assess this and to provide feedback about the group for use with future groups (see Table 9.1).

Even though some group members may have stopped binge eating entirely by now, we tell them to expect relapses. We define the relapse in positive terms, in that it is a cue that they need to work on something, that they need to practice their new skills. We point out that progress seldom goes in a straight line but has its ups and downs. Above all, we tell them not to panic when they relapse. They are to see each relapse as an opportunity to come up with new coping skills. They are not to engage in all-or-nothing thinking such as ''I messed up—I guess I will never be able to give up binge eating.'' Relapsing does not take away the progress they have made so far. It is a cue to review their skills and nourish themselves in ways that do not require food.

We also encourage them to refer to their notes frequently and to reread them from time to time. We ask them to continue filling out the binge-

Table 9.1. Group Evaluation Form

Name _____   Date _____

1. What changes have occurred in your eating habits since you started the group?

2. What other changes have you noticed in yourself since the beginning of the group?

3. Please indicate whether there has been an increase, decrease, or no change in the following behaviors since you started the group:

	DECREASE	NO CHANGE	INCREASE
Number of binges	_____	_____	_____
Number of purges after binge eating	_____	_____	_____
Amount of caloric intake with each binge	_____	_____	_____
Length of binge	_____	_____	_____
Eating three meals a day	_____	_____	_____
Weighing self daily	_____	_____	_____
Number of whole days with no binge	_____	_____	_____
Using coping responses other than binge eating	_____	_____	_____

4. What aspects of the group did you find most valuable?

5. What did you find least valuable?

6. Please rate the following topics in terms of how helpful they were to you:

	VERY HELPFUL	SOMEWHAT HELPFUL	NOT HELPFUL
Bulimic Basics	_____	_____	_____
Health Hazards	_____	_____	_____
Alternative Coping Responses	_____	_____	_____
Changing the Way You Think	_____	_____	_____
Fat Facts	_____	_____	_____
Strategies for Confronting a Binge	_____	_____	_____
Perfectionism ("I shoulds")	_____	_____	_____
Nourishing Yourself Without Food	_____	_____	_____
Ego Tripping	_____	_____	_____
Assertiveness ("yes" & "no")	_____	_____	_____

(continued)

Table 9.1. Group Evaluation Form (*continued*)

	VERY HELPFUL	SOMEWHAT HELPFUL	NOT HELPFUL
Anger			
Societal Pressures to Be Thin			
Body Image			
Binge Diary			

7. What topics would you have liked to see added to the group?

8. Would you recommend this group to anyone else? Why or why not?

9. What suggestions do you have for future groups?

10. What kind of additional help do you think you will need after this group?

11. Additional comments:

purge diary and to use the alternative coping responses. We schedule a follow-up session for 10 weeks following the end of the group. We usually end the group with a closing exercise in which every woman tells each group member what she perceives that woman has given to the group and what kind of gift she would like to give that person. This helps group members to say "goodbye." It also reinforces the gains made in the group so far and suggests future directions for each individual. For example, "You have given this group courage for trying new behaviors even though you were afraid, and if I could give you a gift, I would give you the ability to see your beauty from within and without as others see you."

In the follow-up session, we again review each member's progress, work on current problems, and suggest further directions for growth.

SUMMARY

1. Discuss the homework from the last session. How did others react to the changes in appearance other than weight and the exaggeration of attractive behaviors?
2. Review each person's progress and what changes she sees in herself and others. You may wish to give the Group Evaluation Form (see Table 9.1) to help them assess changes and future directions.
3. Prepare them for relapses.
4. Schedule a follow-up session and ask them to continue filling out the binge diary.
5. Do a closure exercise to help them say "goodbye."

Appendix

WEEKLY BINGE DIARY

Name _____   Week No. _____

	TIME	WHAT I ATE	FEELINGS AND THOUGHTS PRIOR TO EATING	ALTERNATIVE COPING SKILLS
Monday				
Tuesday				
Wednesday				
Thursday				

Name _____ Week No. _____

	TIME	WHAT I ATE	FEELINGS AND THOUGHTS PRIOR TO EATING	ALTERNATIVE COPING SKILLS
Friday				
Saturday				
Sunday				

Total number of binges this week _____
Total number of purges this week _____

References

Abraham, S. F., & Beumont, P. J. V. (1982). How patients describe bulimia or binge eating. *Psychological Medicine, 12,* 625–635.

Alberti, R. E., & Emmons, M. L. (1970). *Your perfect right: A guide to assertive behavior.* San Luis Obispo, CA: Impact.

Alderdissen, R., Florin, I., & Rost, W. (1981). Psychological characteristics of women with bulimia nervosa (bulimarexia). *Behavioural Analysis and Modification, 4,* 314–317.

American Psychiatric Association. (1980). *Diagnostic and statistical manual of mental disorders* (3rd ed.). Washington, DC: Author.

Barbach, L. (1975). *For yourself: The fulfillment of female sexuality.* New York: Doubleday.

Barbach, L. (1980). *Women discover orgasm.* New York: Free Press.

Beck, A. T. (1967). *Depression: Causes and treatments.* Philadelphia, PA: University of Pennsylvania Press.

Beck, A. T., Ward, C. H., Mendelson, M., Mock, J. E., & Erbaugh, J. (1961). An inventory for measuring depression. *Archives of General Psychiatry, 4,* 561–571.

Berkman, L. F., & Syne, S. L. (1979). Social networks, host resistance and mortality: A 9 year follow-up study of Alameda County residents. *American Journal of Epidemiology, 109,* 186–204.

Berzon, B., Pious, G., & Parson, R. (1963). The therapeutic event in group psychotherapy: A study of subjective reports by group members. *Journal of Individual Psychology, 19,* 204–212.

Beumont, P. J. V., George, G. C. W., & Smart, D. E. (1976). "Dieters" and "vomiters and purgers" in anorexia nervosa. *Psychological Medicine, 6,* 617–622.

Bo-Linn, G. W., Santa Ana, C., Morawski, S., & Fordtran, J. (1983). Purging and caloric absorption in bulimic patients and normal women. *Annals of Internal Medicine, 99,* 14–17.

Boskind-Lodahl, M. (1976). Cinderella's stepsisters: A feminist perspective on anorexia nervosa and bulimia. *Signs' Journal of Women in Culture and Society, 2,* 342–356.

Boskind-Lodahl, M., & Sirlin, J. (1977, March). The gorging-purging syndrome. *Psychology Today,* pp. 50–52, 82–85.

Boskind-Lodahl, M., & White, W. C. Jr. (1978). The definition and treatment of bulimarexia in college women: A pilot study. *Journal of the American College Health Association, 27,* 84–86, 97.

Boskind-White, M., & White, W. C. Jr. (1983). *Bulimarexia: The binge/purge cycle.* New York: W. W. Norton.

Bruch, H. (1973). *Eating disorders: Obesity, anorexia nervosa and the person within.* New York: Basic Books.

Burns, D. (1980, November). The perfectionist's script for self-defeat. *Psychology Today,* pp. 34–52.

Casper, R. C., Eckert, E. D., Halmi, K. A., Goldberg, S. C., & Davis, J. M. (1980). Bulimia: Its incidence and clinical importance in patients with anorexia nervosa. *Archives of General Psychiatry, 37,* 1030–1035.

Coffman, D. A. (1984). A clinically derived treatment model for the binge-purge syndrome. In R. C. Hawkins II, W. J. Fremouw, & P. F. Clement (Eds.), *The binge-purge syndrome* (pp. 211–226). New York: Springer.

Coyne, J. C., Aldwin, C. A., & Lazarus, R. S. (1981). Depression and coping in stressful episodes. *Journal of Abnormal Psychology, 5,* 439–447.

Crowther, J. H., Lingswiler, V. M., & Stephens, M. P. (1983). *The topography of binge eating.* Paper presented at the 17th annual convention of the Association for the Advancement of Behavior Therapy, Washington, DC.

Derogatis, L. R., Lipman, R. S., & Covi, L. (1973). SCL-90: An outpatient rating scale. *Psychopharmacology Bulletin, 9,* 13–26.

Dunn, P. K., & Ondercin, P. (1981). Personality variables related to compulsive eating in college women. *Journal of Clinical Psychology, 37,* 43–49.

Fairburn, C. G. (1980). Self-induced vomiting. *Journal of Psychosomatic Research, 24,* 193–197.

Fairburn, C. G. (1981). A cognitive behavioural approach to the treatment of bulimia. *Psychological Medicine, 11,* 707–711.

Fairburn, C. G. (1982). Binge eating and its management. *British Journal of Psychiatry, 141,* 631–633.

Fairburn, C. G., & Cooper, P. J. (1982). Self-induced vomiting and bulimia nervosa: An undetected problem. *British Medical Journal, 284,* 1153–1155.

Garfinkel, P. E., & Garner, D. M. (1982). *Anorexia nervosa: A multidimensional perspective.* New York: Brunner/Mazel.

Garfinkel, P. E., Moldofsky, H., & Garner, D. M. (1980). The heterogeneity of anorexia nervosa: Bulimia as a distinct subgroup. *Archives of General Psychiatry, 37,* 1036–1040.

Garner, D. M., & Bemis, K. M. (1982). A cognitive-behavioral approach to anorexia nervosa. *Cognitive Therapy and Research, 6*(2), 123–150.

Garner, D. M., & Garfinkel, D. E. (1979). The eating attitudes test: An index of the symptoms of anorexia nervosa. *Psychological Medicine, 9,* 273–279.

Goldberg, S. C., Halmi, K. A., Eckert, E. D., Casper, R. C., Davis, J. M., & Roper, M. J. (1978). Short-term prognosis in anorexia nervosa. *Colloquim Int. Neuropsychopharmacologicum,* Vienna, Austria.

Goldberg, S. C., Halmi, K. A., Eckert, E. D., Casper, R. C., Davis, J. M., & Roper, M. J. (1980). Attitudinal dimensions in anorexia nervosa. *Journal of Psychiatric Research, 15,* 239–251.

Gormally, J. (1984). The obese binge eater: Diagnosis, etiology, and clinical issues. In Hawkins II, R. C., Fremouw, W. J., & Clement, P. F. (Eds.), *The binge-purge syndrome* (pp. 47–73). New York: Springer.

Green, R. S., & Rau, J. H. (1974). Treatment of compulsive eating disturbances with anticonvulsant medication. *American Journal of Psychiatry, 131,* 428–432.

Greenway, F. L., Dahms, W. T., & Bray, G. A. (1977). Phenytoin as a treatment of obesity associated with compulsive eating. *Current Therapeutic Research, 21,* 338–342.

Grinc, G. A. (1982). A cognitive-behavioral model for the treatment of chronic vomiting. *Journal of Behavioral Medicine, 5,* 135–141.

Halmi, K. A., Falk, J. R., & Schwartz, E. (1981). Binge eating and vomiting: A survey of a college population. *Psychological Medicine, 11,* 697–706.

Hatsukami, D., Owen, P., Pyle, R., & Mitchell, J. (1982). Similarities and differences on the MMPI between women with bulimia and women with alcohol or drug abuse problems. *Addictive Behaviors, 7,* 435–439.

Hawkins, II, R. C. (1982). *Binge eating as coping behavior: Theory and treatment implications.* Unpublished manuscript, University of Texas, Austin.

Hawkins, II, R. C., & Clement, P. F. (1980). Development and construct validation of a self-report measure of binge eating tendencies. *Addictive Behaviors, 5,* 219–226.

Hawkins, II, R. C., & Clement, P. F. (1984). Binge eating: Measurement problems and a conceptual model. In R. C. Hawkins, II, Fremouw, W. J. & Clement, P. F. (Eds.), *The binge-purge syndrome.* (pp. 229–251). New York: Springer.

Herman, C. P., & Polivy, J. (1978). Restrained eating. In A. J. Stunkard (Ed.), *Obesity* (pp. 208–225). Philadelphia, PA: Saunders.

Herzog, D. B. (1982). Bulimia: The secretive syndrome. *Psychosomatics, 23,* 481–483, 487.

Holmes, T. H., & Rahe, R. H. (1967). The social readjustment rating scale. *Journal of Psychosomatic Research, 11,* 213–218.

House, R. C., Grisius, R., & Bliziotes, M. M. (1981). Perimolysis: Unveiling the surreptitious vomiter. *Oral Surgery, 51,* 152–155.

Hudson, J. I., Laffer, P. S., & Pope, H. G. (1982). Bulimia related to affective disorder by family history and response to the dexamethasone suppression test. *American Journal of Psychiatry, 139,* 685–687.

Johnson, C., & Berndt, D. J. (1983). Preliminary investigation of bulimia and life adjustment. *American Journal of Psychiatry, 140*(6), 774–777.

Johnson, C., Connors, M., & Stuckey, M. (1983). Short-term group treatment of bulimia. *International Journal of Eating Disorders, 2*(4), 199–208.

Johnson, C., & Larson, R. (1982). Bulimia: An analysis of moods and behavior. *Psychosomatic Medicine, 44*(4), 341–351.

Johnson, C. L., Lewis, C., Love, S., Lewis, L., & Stuckey, M. (1983). *Incidence and correlates of bulimic behavior in a female high school population.* Manuscript submitted for publication.

Johnson, C. L., Stuckey, M. K., Lewis, L. D., & Schwartz, D. M. (1982). Bulimia: A descriptive study of 316 cases. *International Journal of Eating Disorders, 2*(1), 3–16.

Johnson, W. G., Schlundt, D. G., Kelley, M. L., & Ruggiero, L. (1984). Exposure with response prevention and energy regulation in the treatment of bulimia. *International Journal of Eating Disorders, 3,* 37–46.

Jones, R. G. (1968). *A factored measure of Ellis' irrational belief systems.* Kansas: Test Systems, Inc.

Katzman, M. A. (1982). *Bulimia and binge eating in college women: A comparison of eating patterns and personality characteristics.* Paper presented at the 16th annual convention of the Association for the Advancement of Behavior Therapy, Los Angeles, CA.

Katzman, M. A. (1984). *A comparison of coping strategies between bulimic, binge eater, depressed and control groups.* (Doctoral dissertation, Arizona State University) *Dissertation Abstracts International,* **45,** 0000A.

Katzman, M. A., & Wolchik, S. A. (1983a). *Behavioral and emotional antecedents and consequences of binge eating in bulimic and binge eating college women.* Paper presented at Eastern Psychological Association, Philadelphia, PA.

Katzman, M. A., & Wolchik, S. A. (1983b). *An empirically based conceptual model for the development of bulimia.* Paper presented at the Western Psychological Association, San Francisco.

Katzman, M. A., & Wolchik, S. A. (1984). Bulimia and binge eating in college women: A comparison of personality and behavioral characteristics. *Journal of Consulting and Clinical Psychology, 52,* 423–428.

Katzman, M. A., Wolchik, S. A., & Braver, S. L. (1984). The prevalence of frequent binge eating and bulimia in a nonclinical college sample. *International Journal of Eating Disorders, 3,* 53–62.

Kenny, F. T., & Solyom, L. (1971). The treatment of compulsive vomiting through faradic disruption of mental images. *Canadian Medical Association Journal, 105,* 1071–1073.

Kurtz, R. (1969). Sex differences and variations in body attitudes. *Journal of Consulting and Clinical Psychology, 33,* 625–629.

Lacey, J. H. (1982). The bulimic syndrome at normal body weight: Reflections on pathogenesis and clinical features. *International Journal of Eating Disorders, 2*(1), 59–66.

Lacey, J. H. (1983). Bulimia nervosa, binge eating, and psychogenic vomiting: A controlled treatment study and long term outcome. *British Medical Journal, 286*, 1609–1613.

Lachar, D. (1974). *The MMPI: Clinical assessment and automated interpretation.* Los Angeles: Western Psychological Services.

Leitenberg, H., Gross, J., Peterson, J., & Rosen, J. (1984). Analysis of an anxiety model and the process of change during exposure plus response prevention treatment of bulimia nervosa. *Behavior Therapy, 15*, 3–20.

Leon, G. R., Carroll, K., Chernyk, B., & Finn, S. (1985). Binge eating and associated habit patterns within college student and identified bulimic populations. *International Journal of Eating Disorders, 4*, 43–47.

Levenson, R. W., & Gottman, J. M. (1978). Toward the assessment of social competence. *Journal of Consulting and Clinical Psychology, 46*, 453–462.

Levin, P. A., Falko, J. M., Dixon, K., & Gallup, E. M. (1980). Benign parotid enlargement in bulimia. *Annals of Internal Medicine, 93*, 827–829.

Linden, W. (1980). Multi-component behavior therapy in a case of compulsive binge-eating followed by vomiting. *Journal of Behavior Therapy and Experimental Psychiatry, 11*, 297–300.

Long, C. G., & Cordle, C. J. (1982). Psychological treatment of binge-eating and self-induced vomiting. *British Journal of Medical Psychology, 55*, 139–145.

Loro, A. D., Jr., & Orleans, C. S. (1981). Binge eating in obesity: Preliminary findings and guidelines for behavioral analysis and treatment. *Addictive Behaviors, 6*, 155–166.

Metropolitan Life Insurance Company of New York. (1983). *New weight standards for males and females.* New York: Author.

Mitchell, J. E., & Pyle, R. L. (1981). The bulimic syndrome in normal weight individuals: A review. *International Journal of Eating Disorders, 1*, 61–73.

Mitchell, J. E., Pyle, R. L., & Eckert, E. D. (1981). Frequency and duration of binge-eating episodes in patients with bulimia. *American Journal of Psychiatry, 138*, 835–836.

Mitchell, J. E., Pyle, R. L., & Miner, R. A. (1982). Gastric dilatation as a complication of bulimia. *Psychosomatics, 23*, 96–97.

Mizes, J. S. (1983). *Bulimia: A review of its symptomatology and treatment.* Unpublished manuscript, North Dakota State University, Fargo.

Mizes, J. S., & Lohr, J. M. (1983). The treatment of bulimia (binge-eating and self-induced vomiting): A quasiexperimental investigation of the effects of stimulus narrowing, self-reinforcement, and self-control relaxation. *International Journal of Eating Disorders, 2*, 59–63.

Morris, K. T., & Shelton, R. L. (1974). *A handbook of verbal group exercises.* Springfield, IL: Charles C Thomas.

Nisbett, R. D. (1972). Hunger, obesity, and the ventro-medial hypothalamus. *Psychological Review, 79*, 433–453.

Novaco, R. A. (1975). *Anger control: The development and evaluation of an experimental treatment.* Lexington, MA: D. C. Heath.

Nowicki, S., & Strickland, B. R. (1973). A locus of control scale for children. *Journal of Consulting and Clinical Psychology, 40*, 148–154.

O'Neill, G. W. (1982). *A systematic desensitization approach to bulimia.* Paper presented at the 16th annual convention of the Association for the Advancement of Behavior Therapy, Los Angeles.

Orbach, S. (1978). *Fat is a feminist issue.* New York: Paddington Press.

Ondercin, P. A. (1979). Compulsive eating in college women. *Journal of College Student Personnel, 20*, 153–157.

Palmer, R. L. (1979). The dietary chaos syndrome: A useful new term? *British Journal of Medical Psychology, 52*, 187–190.

Piers, E. V., & Harris, D. B. (1969). The Piers-Harris children's self-concept scale. Nashville, TN: Counselor Recordings and Tests.

Pope, H. C., Hudson, J. I., Jonas, J. M., & Yurgelun-Todd, D. (1983). Bulimia treated with imipramine: A placebo-controlled, double-blind study. *American Journal of Psychiatry, 140*(5), 554–558.

Pyle, R. L., Mitchell, J. E., & Eckert, E. D. (1981). Bulimia: A report of 34 cases. *Journal of Clinical Psychiatry, 42,* 60–64.

Pyle, R. L., Mitchell, J. E., Eckert, E. D., Halvorson, P. A., Neuman, P. A., & Goff, G. M. (1983). The incidence of bulimia in college freshmen students. *International Journal of Eating Disorders, 2,* 75–85.

Rachman, S., & Hodgson, R. (1980). *Obsessions and compulsions.* Englewood Cliffs, NJ: Prentice-Hall.

Rosen, T. C., & Leitenberg, H. (1982). Bulimia nervosa: Treatment with exposure and response prevention. *Behavior Therapy, 13,* 117–124.

Rosenberg, M. (1979). *Conceiving the self.* New York: Basic Books.

Ross, S. M., Todt, E. H., & Rindflesh, M. A. (1983). Evidence for an anorexic/bulimic MMPI profile. Paper presented at the annual convention of the Rocky Mountain Psychological Association, Salt Lake City, UT.

Rost, W., Neuhaus, M., & Florin, I. (1982). Bulimia nervosa: Sex role attitude, sex role behavior, and sex role related locus of control in bulimarexic women. *Journal of Psychosomatic Research, 26*(4), 403–408.

Roth, G. (1982). *Feeding the hungry heart.* New York: Bobbs-Merrill.

Roy-Byrne, P., Lee-Benner, K., & Yager, J. (1984). Group therapy for bulimia. *International Journal of Eating Disorders, 3*(2), 97–117.

Ruff, G. (1982). *Toward the assessment of body image.* Paper presented at the 16th annual convention of the Association for Advancement of Behavior Therapy, Los Angeles, CA.

Russell, G. (1979). Bulimia nervosa: An ominous variant of anorexia nervosa. *Psychological Medicine, 9,* 429–448.

Smith, M. (1975). *When I say no, I feel guilty.* New York: Dial Press.

Spence, J. T., & Helmreich, R. L. (1978). *Masculinity and femininity: Their psychological dimensions, correlates, and antecedents.* Austin, TX: University of Texas Press.

Stangler, R. S., & Prinz, A. M. (1980). DSM-III: Psychiatric diagnosis in a university population. *American Journal of Psychiatry, 137,* 937–940.

Stunkard, A. J. (1959). Eating patterns and obesity. *Psychiatric Quarterly, 33,* 284–295.

Walsh, T., Stewart, J. W., Wright, L., Harrison, W., Roose, S., & Glassman, A. (1982). Treatment of bulimia with monoamine oxidase inhibitors. *American Journal of Psychiatry, 139*(12), 1629–1630.

Weiss, L., & Katzman, M. K. (1984). Group treatment for bulimic women. *Arizona Medicine, 41*(2), 100–104.

Weiss, S. R., & Ebert, M. H. (1983). Psychological and behavioral characteristics of normal-weight bulimics and normal-weight controls. *Psychosomatic Medicine, 45,* 293–303.

Weiss, T., & Levitz, L. (1976). Diphenylhydantoin treatment of bulimia. *American Journal of Psychiatry, 133,* 1093.

Wermuth, B. M., Davis, K. L., Hollister, L. E., & Stunkard, A. J. (1977). Phenytoin treatment of the binge-eating syndrome. *American Journal of Psychiatry, 134,* 1249–1253.

White, W. C., Jr., & Boskind-White, M. (1981). An experiential-behavioral approach to the treatment of bulimarexia. *Psychotherapy: Theory, Research and Practice, 18,* 501–507.

Wilson, G. T. (1978). Methodological considerations in treatment outcome research on obesity. *Journal of Consulting and Clinical Psychology, 46,* 687–702.

Wolchik, S. A., Weiss, L., & Katzman, M. K. (in press). An empirically validated, short term psycho-educational group treatment program for bulimia. *International Journal of Eating Disorders.*

Wooley, O. W., & Wooley, S. C. (1982). The Beverly Hills eating disorder: The mass market-
ing of anorexia nervosa. *International Journal of Eating Disorders, 1,* 57–69.

Wooley, S. C., & Wooley, O. W. (1981). Overeating as substance abuse. In N. Mello (Ed.).
Advances in substance abuse: Vol. 2. (pp. 41–67). Greenwich, CT: JAI Press.

Yalom, I. D. (1970). *Theory and practice of group psychotherapy.* New York: Basic Books.

Author Index

Subject Index

About the Authors

Lillie Weiss received her PhD in clinical psychology at the State University of New York at Buffalo. She is a psychologist in private practice, Adjunct Associate Professor in the Department of Psychology at Arizona State University, and President of the Maricopa Psychological Society. She was formerly Director of the Eating Disorders Program at Good Samaritan Medical Center in Phoenix, Arizona. Melanie Katzman received her PhD in clinical psychology from Arizona State University and is currently working at the Eating Disorder Institute of The New York Hospital—Cornell Medical Center (Westchester Division). Sharlene Wolchik received her PhD in clinical psychology from Rutgers University and is currently Associate Professor in the Department of Psychology at Arizona State University.

Psychology Practitioner Guidebook

Editors
Arnold P. Goldstein, Syracuse University
Leonard Krasner, SUNY at Stony Brook
Sol L. Garfield, Washington University

Elsie M. Pinkston & Nathan L. Linsk–*CARE OF THE ELDERLY: A Family Approach*

Donald Meichenbaum–*STRESS INOCULATION TRAINING*

Sebastiano Santostefano–*COGNITIVE CONTROL THERAPY WITH CHILDREN AND ADOLESCENTS*

Lillie Weiss, Melanie Katzman & Sharlene Wolchik–*TREATING BULIMIA: A Psychoeducational Approach*

Edward B. Blanchard & Frank Andrasik–*MANAGEMENT OF CHRONIC HEADACHES: A Psychological Approach*

Raymond G. Romanczyk–*CLINICAL UTILIZATION OF MICROCOMPUTER TECHNOLOGY*

Philip H. Bornstein & Marcy T. Bornstein–*MARITAL THERAPY: A Behavioral-Communications Approach*